Relaxation and the Pursuit of Wellbeing

A guidebook for addressing the stress
and anxiety of everyday life

David Thomas, PHD

Copyright © 2020, David Thomas

Copyright © 2020 by David Thomas, PhD

All rights reserved. No part of this publication may be reproduced, stored in a retrieval system, or transmitted, in any form or by any means, electronic, mechanical, photocopying, recording, or otherwise, without the prior written permission of the author.

ISBN: 9780578710846

Distributed by IngramSpark and Fifty-Six Street Press

Cover art: Paula Ziegman

Cover design: David Thomas

Printed in the United States of America

An earlier version of this book served as my dissertation. The current version is designed for use by individuals, therapists, counselors, and trainers. The book can be ordered through local booksellers. Contact the author at: dtec@cox.net

For
L. Keith Miller

TABLE OF CONTENTS

TABLE OF CONTENTS   5

ACKNOWLEDGEMENTS   7

INTRODUCTION   9

CHAPTER I – Profound Relaxation: Definition & Rationale   11

What is profound relaxation? Why learn profound relaxation?

Study Guide	15
Exercise A: Social Readjustment Rating Scale	17
Exercise B: Stress-Induced Symptoms and Disorders	19
Progress Check	21

CHAPTER II – Profound Relaxation: Procedures, Sensations & State of Mind   23

The relaxation script. Why focus training on the muscles? Sensations accompanying relaxation. Passive concentration.

Study Guide	28
Exercise C: Developing a Relaxation Schedule	32
Exercise D: Evaluating a Relaxation Session	34
Progress Check	36

CHAPTER III – Differential Relaxation: Definition & Rationale   39

The wisdom of the body. The "Noise Machine". Scanning the inner environment. Differential relaxation. Deliberate living.

Study Guide	46
Exercise E: Proper Bodily Posture	49
Exercise F: Building the Will: Mini-Challenges	52
Progress Check	55

CHAPTER IV – Identifying Anxiety-Inducing Factors   57

Situational factors. Social factors. Personal factors.

Study Guide	64
Exercise G: Social Support Network	67
Exercise H: Lovers & Teachers	70
Exercise I: Communication Style	71
Exercise J: Personality Characteristics	74
Exercise K: Lifestyle Considerations	75
Progress Check	77

CHAPTER V – Pain Drains, Addiction and the Heroic Strategy   79

Pain drains. Addiction. The heroic strategy. Concept formation. Social responsibility.

    Study Guide   88
    Exercise L: Pain Drains & Addictions   91
    Exercise M: Forgiveness   92
    Exercise N: Choice and Responsibility   95
    Exercise O: Sharing Your Gifts   97
    Progress Check   98

REFERENCES   101

APPENDIX A: Answer Key for Progress Checks   107

APPENDIX B: Relaxation Instructions   109

APPENDIX C: Profound Relaxation – A Thirty-Day Schedule   115

ACKNOWLEDGEMENTS

My sincere thanks to the following individuals:

Drs. Johann Stoyva and Thomas Budzynski from whom, while working in their biofeedback laboratory at the University of Colorado Medical Center, I learned much about the relationship between relaxation, lifestyle, and stress-related disease;

Dr. L. Keith Miller from whom I learned the science and art of Applied Behavior Analysis and with whom I spent innumerable hours discussing the issues in this book; and finally,

Dr. John Poole, Dr. Leland Kaiser, Dr. Ray Foster, Dr. David Finks, Dr. Donald Stilson, Dr. Montrose Wolf, Dr. William Tuttle, and Dr. Paul Schumaker with whom I have had many hours of discussion concerning this project and from whom I received invaluable feedback and support.

—David Thomas, PhD
November 2020

INTRODUCTION

"Which ship goes most often onto the rocks . . . the drifting ship or the ship with a pilot?"
George Bernard Shaw

The purpose of this book is twofold: first, to teach "profound relaxation," an extremely useful skill and for most people, an easy one to learn; and second, to discuss "differential relaxation", the relaxation of everyday life.

The first two chapters focus on profound relaxation. Their purpose is to teach you to relax deeply—body and mind—in a single session of fifteen to twenty minutes. Like meditation, profound relaxation is considered an anti-stress response as it leads to an overall calming or quieting of the nervous system. If practiced daily, profound relaxation can reduce your vulnerability to a wide array of stress-related symptoms and disorders.

In addition to profound relaxation, this book—beginning with Chapter 3—introduces the notion of differential relaxation, what might be called the "at ease with yourself" mode of relaxation. Differential relaxation is not so much a skill as it is a way of being and doing. It means: *Using only the tension and energy required to perform a given act properly, not over-doing and not forcing.*

Achieving the differentially relaxed mode of relaxation is not easy. It can be difficult. This book is written with an appreciation of how difficult it can be, but also with faith in the individual's capacity to put right the factors that must be addressed if relaxation is to occur. The basic assumption here is that everyone wants to be at ease with themselves, to feel good about their worth as a human being whether alone or in the presence of others. And thus, that everyone, at a deep and fundamental level, is motivated to do what they can to rid themselves of the tension and anxiety that threatens health and limits self-expression.

Of course, if the going gets tough, as it might from time to time (there are sometimes difficult issues with which we must contend before we can relax), there is wisdom in seeking professional help. Indeed, one use of this book is with therapists or counselors working with clients committed to addressing the sources of their anxiety.

Finally, the one and only proviso accompanying this book is a simple one. If you attempt to proceed with the training regimen detailed in this book and find that you are unable to stay with it, stopping and starting and stopping again, *don't worry about it.* Much progress is made in an up-two-back-one pattern. If you have dropped the effort, chances are you will come back to it. Reading this book, reading it without begrudging the time spent, suggests that you already embrace one of the tenets on which this book is based; namely, that your everyday experience is most meaningful, most full, most joyful, when you are in charge of it, when you are choosing it and in a position to choose differently as the need to do so arises. It is, after all, the drifting ship and not the ship with a pilot that goes most often onto the rocks. To drift along, to pretend that someone else is in charge and that you lack the capacity to choose your own course, is uncomfortable, risky, perhaps even disastrous in some cases, a fact that you sense rather deeply or you would not be reading books of this sort. So, if you fall off the program, be easy on yourself. The knowledge that has created an interest in this material will bring you back to this book or to others like it. And what you will discover as you proceed is what you may already suspect: relaxation—*being at ease with yourself*—is both an aid to and an outcome of the successful navigation of everyday life.

CHAPTER I

Profound Relaxation: Definition & Rationale

"To relax is, of course, the first thing a dancer has to learn. It is also the first thing a patient has to learn when he confronts the analyst. It is the first thing any one has to learn in order to live."
                                        Henry Miller

WHAT IS PROFOUND RELAXATION?

Profound relaxation is characterized by three things: first, *the absence of muscular tension.* All movement requires muscular tension. Arm and leg muscles tighten in order for us to lift; neck muscles tighten in order for us to turn our heads; chest, throat, tongue, and jaw muscles tighten in order for us to speak. Even thought, the simple process of talking inaudibly to ourselves requires some muscular tension. Edmund Jacobson, developer of Progressive Relaxation, wrote:

> ". . . when you imagine or recall or reflect about anything, you tense muscles somewhere, as if you were actually doing something, but to a much slighter degree. If you relax these particular tensions, you cease to imagine or recall or reflect about the matter in question—for instance, a matter of worry."[1]

Profound relaxation means the absence of even *these particular tensions,* the tensions of the throat, jaws, tongue, lips, eyes, forehead, and scalp.

Second, profound relaxation is characterized by *an increase in peripheral blood flow.* When you are profoundly relaxed, the blood is found in the extremities, near the surface, circulating throughout the smallest capillaries. Notice your hands, for example, prior to being introduced to a group of strangers . . . before a public speaking engagement . . . during a headache . . . when stopped for a traffic violation. All are situations that dramatize the body's response to tension-producing situations. In such situations the blood withdraws to the central veins and cavities where it can meet the demands of the large muscle groups. In profound relaxation the blood is near the surface, on the periphery, where it can cleanse and nourish the surface tissues of feet, hands, fingers, and toes.

Finally, profound relaxation is characterized by a *quiet, non-active mind*—the absence or shutting-off of the normal mental processes which include attending, calculating, discriminating, evaluating. In the profoundly relaxed state, the mind floats freely, secure from the worries and considerations of everyday life. If you've ever experienced an inability to fall asleep because your mind was "going a hundred miles an hour," then you know how an active, restless mind can work against you. Consider also the tension and anxiety that returns when you review an emotion-provoking argument. Profound relaxation is the absence of this sort of arousal-producing mental activity. Instead, it is characterized by a quiet, non-active mind, a mind emptied of emotional content, a calm mind with random thoughts and occasional dream-like images.

WHY LEARN PROFOUND RELAXATION?

Outside the community in which this book is being written is a network of old-fashioned country roads.[2] Following Spring downpours, it is not uncommon to find deep ruts in these roads left behind by the tractors and pick-ups that travel down them; ruts that harden with the summer drought. For the individual out for a Sunday drive, these ruts are difficult to avoid: frequently, the ruts "lock-in" the wheels of the car. When this happens, the country outing, perhaps sought for relaxation and escape, becomes a trap with excessive wear and tear for both driver and car.

This experience has its parallel in modern life. Often we find that we are "locked-in," caught (or so it seems) by a pattern of everyday life that provides little pleasure and can't possibly be sustained. Eventually, the wear and tear of such patterns runs us down. Many who spend their adult lives hampered by tension headaches, migraine headaches, sleep-onset insomnia, high blood pressure, cardiac disturbances, gastrointestinal ailments, anxieties from the specific to the general, experience these stress-related disorders because of the grueling *lock-ins* of their everyday lives.

Examine the characteristics of your everyday life. Perhaps you have a job that no longer holds your interest. You do it now "just for the money." Even so, you seem always to come up short, your bills as difficult as ever to pay, even your leisure time is spent worrying about how to make ends meet. Or, perhaps you are the executive who can never leave work at the office. Your evenings are full of thoughts about the discussions and decisions of the day. How you will handle tomorrow's demands is with you until you fall asleep. Or, perhaps you are home all day, every day, bored beyond description, nothing to look forward to except dinner and decorating the guest room. The number of stressful scenarios is endless. All of us whether blue collar workers, high-powered executives, short-order cooks, or college professors are vulnerable in one way or another to the lock-ins that oppose mental and physical health.

Johann Stoyva, a researcher in the field of stress and anxiety, has illustrated graphically the effect of a highly stressful schedule. Figure 1 shows how over the course of a single day the level of nervousness or bodily activation increases when in the grips of such a schedule.

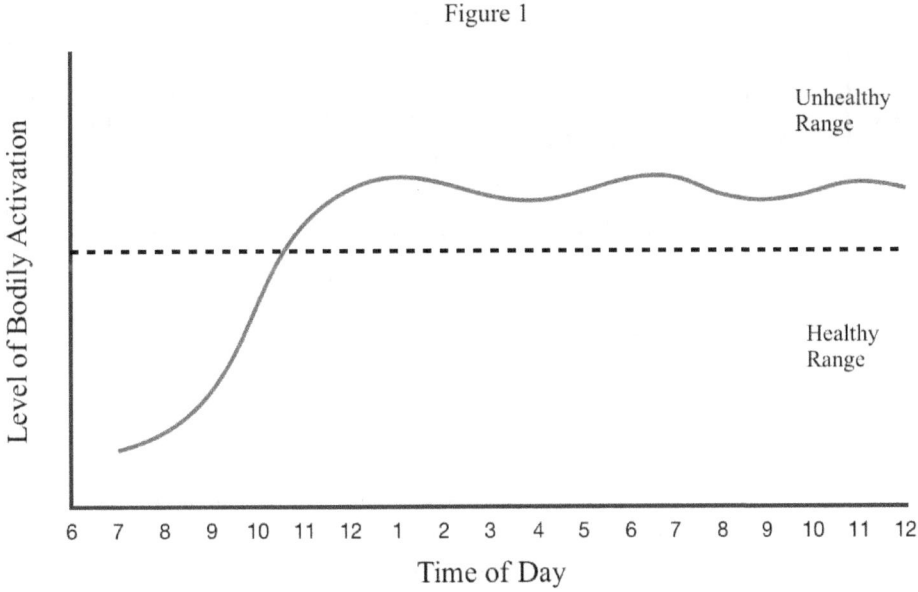

Figure 1

For some, the day may be so demanding that by mid-morning they have gone well beyond a healthy range of bodily activation. They no longer feel calm and relaxed, nor do they feel under control. Instead, they feel rushed. The slightest irritation is magnified out of proportion. They find that they are rude to the very people they most want to treat courteously. In the extreme, their decision-making suffers, as they are unable to focus their full attention. By bedtime, their minds are spinning and their stomachs are churning until nervous exhaustion turns into sleep.

The consequences of a daily pattern similar to this are often disastrous. Sooner or later some part of the body breaks down. Some people, for example, feel stress in their stomachs or intestines in the form of ulcers or spastic bowels; others feel it in their muscles with soreness or headaches; still others feel it in their cardiovascular systems with heart rate arrhythmias and high blood pressure.

Profound relaxation is a *partial* solution to this problem. It offers an "anti-stress response." By engaging in profound relaxation daily, it is possible to combat the damaging effects of excessively stressful schedules. Tom Budzynski, another researcher in the area of stress and anxiety, has illustrated the usefulness of profound relaxation. If at mid-morning, you were to practice profound relaxation (as indicated by the arrow in Figure 2), you would dampen your increasing bodily activation. Another profound relaxation session in the late afternoon or early evening, if necessary, would serve to dampen it again. In this way, the entire day could be negotiated with a considerable reduction in bodily cost.

It should be emphasized, however, that as valuable as profound relaxation is, it is only a partial solution to the problems generated by highly stressful schedules. Simply reducing

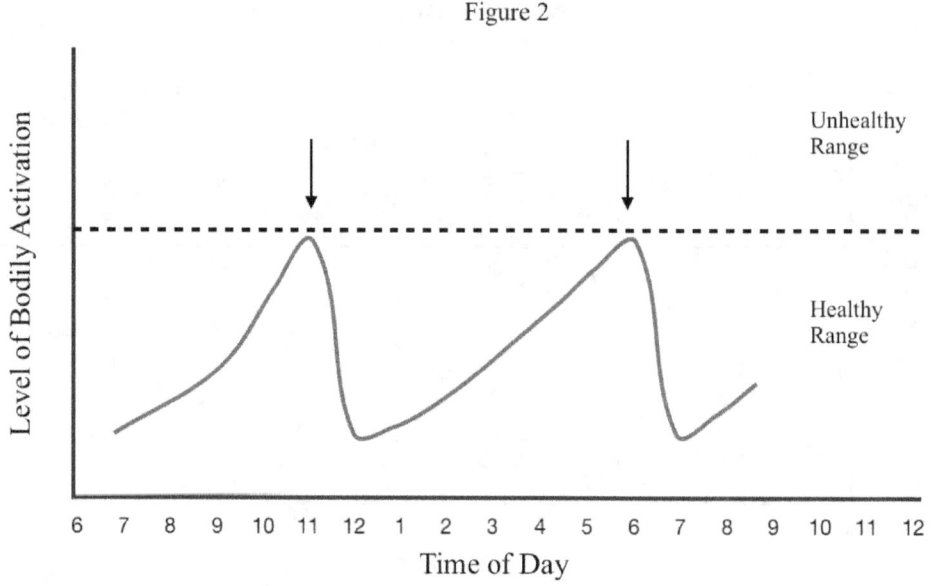

Figure 2

the price you pay does little to change the fact that your schedule is (or may be) out of control and growing more so every day. That remains the problem and as such will cause only trouble until it is in some way addressed.

Consider again the country road analogy. In order to pull out of the hardened ruts, we have to grasp the steering wheel and turn the car toward the smooth and flat portions of the road. What happens next can be discouraging since the car now vibrates and slides more violently than it ever did in the ruts. The inclination may be to turn back; after all, things may not improve once we are out. It's at that point that presence of mind, energy, and acceleration are needed if freedom from the lock-in is to be obtained. Success depends upon the skill of the driver, the condition of the car, and the particular portion of the lock-in selected for escape. The outcome, however, if we are successful, is greater freedom.

The country road analogy illustrates the role played by profound relaxation. To put it simply, profound relaxation will not get you out of the ruts and lock-ins of everyday life. It will, however, reduce the "wear and tear" you experience while in them. Profound relaxation helps you cope, it offers you an anti-stress response. It helps you minimize the strain of a less than optimal daily schedule by giving you a means for combating the stress-related discomforts that accompany such schedules. That is the benefit of profound relaxation and reason enough to practice it. But it also offers more. It leads, if practiced regularly, to an overall calming, to a conservation of energy and hence, to a strengthening and fortifying of the self. That's the key additional value of profound relaxation, the fact that it fortifies you, permitting you to proceed somewhat more calmly and with a clearer mind to a resolution of those issues that bring stress and anxiety into your life. It helps you conserve your energy for when you really need it, and you really need it whenever you elect to address the factors in yourself and in the outer world (the "lock-ins") that threaten your health by imposing stress and anxiety.

STUDY GUIDE / REVIEW

Complete each statement by filling the blank. Return to the text for review as well as to verify the accuracy of your answers.

1. First, profound relaxation means the absence of muscular _____.

2. Second, profound relaxation means _____ peripheral blood flow.

3. Profound relaxation will cleanse and _____ the surface tissues of feet, hands, fingers, and toes.

4. Profound relaxation also means a quiet, non-active _____.

5. Profound relaxation implies the _____ of arousal-producing mental activity.

6. The life pattern that consistently makes demands beyond your capability to deliver extracts your _____ as its price.

7. Another word for "lock-in" is _____.

8. Some lock-ins lead to very stressful schedules, schedules that result in the entire day being spent in the _____ range of bodily activation.

9. Some people feel stress in their cardiovascular system, others feel it in their muscles, and still others feel it in their _____ or intestines.

10. Profound relaxation is not a total _____ to the problems inherent in life's many lock-ins.

11. It offers you a _____ skill.

12. It can be considered an anti-_____ response.

13. By engaging in profound relaxation daily you can combat the damaging effects of _____.

14. The use of profound relaxation means that the entire day can be negotiated with a considerable _____ in bodily cost.

15. Profound relaxation will make you less vulnerable to _____-related disorders.

16. It helps you conserve your _____.

17. Profound relaxation cuts down on the wear and tear; it helps you cope; and it gives you energy for when you really need it, i.e., for when you decide to deal with the issues that are keeping you _____.

*Be sure you have completed all statements accurately
before moving to the exercises.*

EXERCISE A: Life Events Scale

Listed on the following page are forty-three events that bring change into our lives. As you review this list you will notice that some of these "life change events" are dreaded (and dreadful) whereas others are not, e.g., outstanding personal achievement. Yet, to varying degrees, all have one thing in common; all require adjustment, all are disruptions to the everyday routine. Today's world is full of "routine-changing" events, requiring continuous adjustment and considerable flexibility. For when we can no longer adjust, our health and wellness often suffer and we experience, in Hans Selye's phrase, a disorder of adaption.[3]

The purpose of this exercise is to assess the extent to which you have experienced "life-changing" events in recent months and thus, the extent to which you are "at risk" with respect to disorders of adaption.

Directions:

1) Place a checkmark next to those life-change events that have been a part of your life in the past year. Check also those events that you expect will occur within the next month.

2) Add the numbers in parentheses next to your checkmarks. Place the total score on the line at the bottom of the scale.

(NOTE: In one of the studies that developed and validated this scale, it was established that as the total score increased so, too, did the likelihood of illness.[4] Thirty-seven percent of the participants in that study with scores between 150 and 199 suffered from a disease of adaptation within the two-year "at risk" period that followed the clustering of those life-change events. Fifty-one percent experienced a disease of adaptation if they scored between 200 and 299, and of those with scores of 300 or more, 75 percent suffered from such a disease: The higher the score, the greater the likelihood of illness…and—as they also discovered—the higher the score, the more severe the illness. People vary, of course, in their ability to adjust to life-change events. What is disastrous for one person is not so disastrous for another. Not everyone with a high score suffered from a disease of adaptation. But the likelihood does increase: the more life-change events, the more likely that even the most adaptable of individuals will experience a disease of adaptation.

The two-year "at risk" period reflects a reasonable period after which it is safe to assume that adaptation has resulted without illness. The work of Dr. Hans Selye[5] has helped clarify the body's reaction to adaptation requirements. Initially, according to Selye, there is an alarm reaction as the individual reorganizes in an effort to meet the new demand. Then follows a period of resistance as the individual successfully copes. Finally, there occurs the exhaustion phase as the individual no longer is capable of sustaining the internal organization needed to cope. The alarm and exhaustion phases, in particular, are vulnerable periods as the individual is in transition and offering a less organized resistance.)

Social Readjustment Rating Scale[6]

1. Death of a spouse _____ (100)
2. Divorce _____ (73)
3. Marital separation _____ (65)
4. Jail term _____ (63)
5. Death of a close family member _____ (63)
6. Personal injury or illness _____ (53)
7. Marriage _____ (50)
8. Fired at work _____ (47)
9. Marital difficulties _____ (45)
10. Retirement _____ (45)
11. Change in health of family member _____ (44)
12. Pregnancy _____ (40)
13. Sex difficulties _____ (39)
14. Gain of a new family member _____ (39)
15. Business readjustment _____ (39)
16. Change in financial situation _____ (38)
17. Death of a close friend _____ (37)
18. Change to a different line of work _____ (36)
19. Change in number of arguments with spouse _____ (35)
20. Mortgage over $10,000 _____ (31)
21. Foreclosure of mortgage or loan _____ (30)
22. Change in responsibilities at work _____ (29)
23. Son or daughter leaving home _____ (29)
24. Trouble with in-laws _____ (29)
25. Outstanding personal achievement _____ (28)
26. Spouse begins or stops work _____ (26)
27. Begin or end school _____ (26)
28. Change in living conditions _____ (25)
29. Revision of personal habits _____ (24)
30. Trouble with boss _____ (23)
31. Change in work hours or conditions _____ (20)
32. Change in residence _____ (20)
33. Change in school _____ (20)
34. Change in recreation _____ (19)
35. Change in church activities _____ (18)
36. Change in social attitudes _____ (18)
37. Mortgage or loan of less than $10,000 _____ (17)
38. Change in sleeping habits _____ (16)
39. Change in number of family get-togethers _____ (15)
40. Change in eating habits _____ (15)
41. Vacation _____ (13)
42. Christmas _____ (12)
43. Minor violations of the law _____ (11)

Total Score: _____

EXERCISE B: Stress-Induced Symptoms and Disorders

Why is it that a similar cluster of life-change events produces such a variety of stress-related disorders? Why not the same disorder for all people? The answer is that each of us inherits from our parents a unique mix of biological strengths and weaknesses and it is in our weakest bodily part that we first show the signs of excessive stress. For one person, with a highly sensitive cardiovascular system, this can mean the development of heart rate irregularities or high blood pressure while another person, with weakness in the smooth muscles of the lower digestive tract, develops a spastic colon; these differences despite the fact that both individuals lead comparably stressful lives and/or had the same recent clustering of life-change events.

In Exercise B you are asked to review a Checklist of Stress-Induced Symptoms and Disorders. Several of the disorders listed can be the result of factors other than stress. And that fact should be kept in mind. Yet, an argument does exist relating each of these disorders (and one's increasing susceptibility to them) to stress.[7]

There are three reasons for carefully completing Exercise B. First, Exercise B will help you identify your weak "link," the way in which you first display the signs and symptoms of stress. Second, it will help you change your view of these disorders. Instead of seeing them strictly as medical problems with which you will have to learn to live, you can begin to view them—if it seems appropriate—as lifestyle problems. Finally, the score you obtain by completing Exercise B will provide you with a standard against which to compare subsequent scores. If you consistently practice profound relaxation (along perhaps with other health-promoting changes), it is likely that subsequent scores will decrease. Thus, periodically completing Exercise B will help you monitor your progress toward a healthier everyday life.

Directions:

1) Place today's date above the first column to the right of the items

2) Place a 3 in the blank next to those items that you experience one or more times a week. Place a 2 by those items that you experience one or more times a month but less than once a week. Place a 1 by those items that you experience one or more times a year but less than once a month. Place a 0 by those items that you experience less than once a year.

3) Add the numbers you have entered and place the total on the line at the bottom of the column.

4) Re-do the checklist in six to eight weeks and compare your scores. The difference is one measure of your success at modifying the side effects of excessive stress.

Checklist of Stress-Induced Symptoms and Disorders

Date:					
Lump in the throat					
Dry mouth					
Bad taste					
Cold or damp hands					
Cold or smelly feet					
Protrusion of the eyeballs					
Trembling hands					
Tense neck or upper back					
Indigestion					
Nausea					
Heart racing					
Dizziness					
Constipation					
Diarrhea					
Excessive gas					
Excessive urination					
Anal burning or itching					
Anal tear					
Piles (Hemorrhoids)					
Lower back pain					
Cold sore(s)					
Herpes simplex					
Sleep onset insomnia					
Early morning awakenings					
Anxiety					
Upper respiratory infections					
Severe tonsillitis					
Tension headaches					
Migraine headaches					
Hyperventilation					
Severe post-menopausal flushes					
Lower abdominal pain					
Ulcers					
Premature ejaculation					
Secondary impotence					
Sudden weight changes					
Obesity					
Gall-stones					
Rheumatism					
Influenza					
Gout					
Hyperthyroidism					
Diabetes					
Apoplexy					
Arthritis					
Arteriosclerosis					
Depression					
Alcoholism (active)					
Score:					

PROGRESS CHECK

The Progress Check provides you with an opportunity to assess your understanding of the information contained in Chapter I. Answer the questions below as accurately as you can. When you have finished, check your answers with those in the answer key.

1. Define profound relaxation.

   _____
   _____
   _____
   _____
   _____

2. Profound relaxation provides you with what might be called an _____-_____ response.

3. Profound relaxation permits you to _____ more effectively with the stress of everyday life.

4. It promotes a conservation of _____.

5. A cluster of life-change events within a given period of time increases the likelihood of _____.

6. When our adjustment limits are exceeded, we are likely to experience what Hans Selye has called a disorder of _____.

7. The higher your score on the Social Readjustment Rating Scale, the more or less (circle one) likely you are to experience illness.

8. It is important to remember that people vary in their ability to _____ to life-change events.

9. The "at risk" period that follows the clustering of several life-change events is assumed to be _____ years.

10. Each of us inherits a unique mix of biological strengths and _____.

11. It is in our _____ bodily part that we first show the signs of excessive stress.

12. The Checklist of Stress-Induced Symptoms and Disorders helps you identify the ways in which you show the signs of _____.

13. It is important that you learn to view the disorders listed on the Checklist of Stress-Induced Symptoms and Disorders as problems of _____, at least potentially so.

14. If such disorders are to be corrected, at least in part, they require a change in _____.

15. If you consistently practice profound relaxation, then re-doing the Checklist of Stress-Induced Symptoms and Disorders in six weeks should result in a _____ score.

Check your answers against those listed in the Answer Key—Appendix A.

Chapter II

Profound Relaxation: Procedures, Sensations, & State of Mind

The twentieth century saw the development of two disciplines to which this book is particularly indebted. The first is Progressive Relaxation, developed in this country by Edmund Jacobson, and the second is Autogenic Therapy, developed in Germany by Johannes Shultz and Wolfgang Luthe. Evolving in parallel, these disciplines appear to have been motivated by the same desire; namely, to find a treatment for the tension and anxiety disorders already too prevalent in the early years of the twentieth century. An additional concern shared by these disciplines was that their treatment should consist of a set of simple procedures that the individual could apply to him or herself. A substantial literature[1] now exists attesting to their success. The relaxation training script accompanying this book draws extensively on the simple but effective procedures developed by the practitioners of Progressive Relaxation and Autogenic Therapy.

THE RELAXATION SCRIPT

The relaxation script accompanying this book (Appendix B) is designed to help you learn to profoundly relax. Its purpose is twofold: First, to provide you with the experience of profound relaxation; and second, to increase your ability to recognize and eliminate unwanted tension.

The relaxation script contains a sequence of *tense-relax exercises,* each exercise involving a different set of muscles. The first step of each exercise is to *tense or flex* a specific muscle or muscle grouping. During this step you should try to localize the tension in the specific muscle being exercised. Do not allow the tension to spread to other muscles if you can help it. If you are told to *"tighten the muscles of your stomach as though you were about to be hit in the stomach,"* you should try to avoid the buildup of tension in your chest, hips, thighs, and arms. By localizing the tension in your stomach, you will sooner come to recognize the tensions and discomforts associated with a "tight" stomach. The same holds for the other regions of the body. The task of step one is to localize the tension. The task of step two is to *release that tension,* to relax the muscle, allowing the accumulated tension to flow out freely. The goal is to produce a muscle as smooth and as limp as possible while at the same time enjoying the relief accompanying relaxation.

This two-step procedure, of first tensing and then relaxing a given muscle or muscle grouping, will teach you to detect the presence of tension in particular muscles (or muscle groupings). With practice, this procedure will teach you to recognize and then eliminate unwanted tension throughout the body.

The rate at which you acquire this important discrimination (between the muscle when tensed even slightly and the same muscle when fully relaxed) is, in part, a function of how well you are able to *passively* focus your attention. Therefore, throughout each lesson you are encouraged to *"focus on the feelings"* generated by the tensed muscle, to *"make mental contact"* with the sensations coming from the tensed region, to *"feel the relief"* that comes from releasing the tension, and to *"take note of the pleasure"* that emerges as you *"dissolve the discomfort"* associated with the tensed muscle.

Each of these phrases is asking you to ignore momentarily all other thoughts and to note the sensations coming from the specific region being exercised. Success at directing your attention in this fashion will accelerate your learning because it will allow you to recognize the subtle cues associated with the increase and decrease of tension. These cues will become signposts or markers allowing you to map the environment within your body. Once mapped, you will be able to find your own way to deeper states of relaxation.

Following the tense-relax exercises, each session involves a backward counting from five to zero. With each count allow yourself to sink more deeply into relaxation. By the time you reach zero, you will be thoroughly relaxed, profoundly relaxed. All tension will be released and your face will be free of expression. After a period of silence, during which you may enjoy the calmness accompanying deep relaxation, you will be counted back from zero to five. With each count you should allow yourself to become slightly more aroused until by five, you are ready to open your eyes. At that point, you will be instructed to move your fingers and toes, increasing/ensuring circulation. If at the conclusion of the session you don't feel like returning to your tasks immediately, allow yourself a few minutes to recover. *Then ease yourself back.* Your goal is to sustain for as long as you can the calm obtained during the relaxation experience.

WHY FOCUS TRAINING ON THE MUSCLES?

There are three reasons for working extensively with the muscles. First, the muscles constitute "about half the weight of the entire body."[2] This is an important point given that the body is a system of inter-connected and mutually influencing parts. The influence of the musculature spreads rapidly because the muscles comprise a large percentage (50%) of the body's mass. As the muscles relax, they dampen the activation of the entire nervous system. When the muscles are deeply relaxed, it is difficult to experience tension or anxiety in any other region of the body. Even coherent mental activity is hard to sustain when the muscles are relaxed thoroughly. So, by learning how to relax the muscles, you will be learning how to relax the entire body.

The second reason for focusing on the muscles is that we already have, to varying degrees, the ability to detect subtle changes in our level of muscular tension. This is particularly true of our truck and limbs, the parts of our bodies that allow us to accomplish so many of our daily tasks. The sudden shifts in muscle tension required to complete these tasks draws our attention to our muscles and emphasizes for us the difference between the tensed and the relaxed condition. This teaches us to recognize changes in muscular tension and provides us with the very skill we hope to refine and extend, particularly to the muscles of the face.

Finally, training focuses on the muscles because research and experience strongly suggest a link between the level of mental activity and the level of tension in the face. As worry and mental disturbances increase, so too does facial muscle tension. By learning to thoroughly relax the jaws, lips, throat, tongue, eyes, and forehead, you will be learning to shut off your over-active mind. Again, to quote Jacobson:

> ". . . when you imagine or recall or reflect about anything, you tense muscles somewhere, as if you were actually looking or speaking or doing something, but to a much slighter degree. If you relax *these particular tensions,* you cease to imagine or recall or reflect about the matter in question--for instance, a matter of worry."[3]

By learning to detect and then relax subtle changes in facial muscle tension, you will be learning to quiet your over-active mind.

Thus, training focuses on the muscles for three reasons. First, the muscles exert a tremendous influence over the rest of the body—where the muscles lead the rest of the body is likely to follow. Second, to varying degrees we already have the skill we hope to refine; namely, the ability to recognize subtle changes in our level of muscular tension. And third, control over the muscles of the face provides one means for detecting and then shutting off the worry and self-chatter that can rob us of healthful silence and clear thought.

SENSATIONS ACCOMPANYING RELAXATION

The shift from the aroused or activated condition of everyday life to the profoundly relaxed condition produces a number of bodily sensations. It is important to be aware of these sensations, as they are the natural byproduct of your body's shift to a more relaxed state. Allow the sensations to occur and to develop without interference. Enjoy them if you can. They are evidence of your body's movement in the direction of greater relaxation.

For example, as you relax you may notice an increase in saliva and thus, a need to swallow. This indicates that the body has relaxed enough to allow its recuperative and digestive processes to be set in motion. As you proceed, unexpected muscle twitches may occur as pockets of trapped tension in the arms, legs, neck, and back are released. This can be followed by sensations of heaviness in the arms and legs as your muscles take on a "lifeless" quality. The flow of blood to the periphery will be occurring at this time and will be responsible for the sensation of warmth in your hands, arms, feet, and legs. This can lead to a feeling of warmth-all-over and/or to tingling sensations in your fingers and toes.

With your muscles relaxed, you may become aware of what seems like an unusual pounding in your chest. This is because the beating of your heart is not being masked by the tension of your musculature, permitting you to perceive more clearly your heart's signal. For the same reason you may become aware of your breathing as it assumes a slow and rhythmic pattern. These perceptions, as they occur, may be followed by floating or drifting sensations. Your face may seem to soften. You may even feel detached from your body as though you were no longer connected to your trunk and limbs.

As you relax, your mental processes will also be undergoing a gradual change, as well. You may find, for example, that your thoughts have become less organized, that they are flowing along by themselves. Forgotten memories may return only to be followed by a sequence of vivid, though unconnected and fleeting images. These images may be moving and full of action or static, like a series of still photographs. Many will absorb your awareness and leave you, like in a dream, with the sense of having been a part of the image. On some occasions, you may fall asleep.

It's unlikely that you will experience all of these sensations every time you practice profound relaxation. Moreover, you perhaps will never experience some of them. Whichever the case, your reaction to them should be *passive*. If they arouse your "active" interest, they will disappear and be replaced by the sensations that accompany active study and analysis. Note their occurrence, experience them as fully as you can, but don't actively study them and thereby stifle their development. The sensations accompanying profound relaxation are pleasurable. They are your body's way of reinforcing the care and good sense you exhibit by practicing health-enhancing relaxation.

PASSIVE CONCENTRATION

There is a state of mind that facilitates movement into the profoundly relaxed condition. The Autogenic Therapists call it *passive concentration*. Passive concentration refers to a non-aggressive state of mind wherein you respond to thoughts, feelings and sensations with utter detachment. In passive concentration, rather than trying to be "in control," you simply "let yourself be."[4]

Few of us experience this state of mind with any regularity but we all have had glimpses of it. Sidney Jourard, a psychologist interested in the "letting yourself be" state of mind, points to a common experience that helps define this passive mode of experiencing.

> " . . . When one has soaked oneself for half an hour or so in a hot bath, one becomes extremely limp, relaxed and passive. One's thoughts, so long as one does not fall asleep, are most likely to drift or play, without conscious direction. If that is the case, then one is letting himself be. In the state of letting be, the individual does not seek to steer, guide, or direct each thought as it arises, but instead permits it to arise and be followed by whatever thought, image, or memory comes next."[5]

When in the passive concentration mode, you are never called to action by your own thoughts. Instead, they are allowed to parade by without the power to take you with them. You remain relaxed, unattached to their meaning, in dramatic contrast to the concentration required in the work-a-day world.

In the work-a-day world, we are called upon to concentrate on the ideas, plans, and tasks associated with our goals. Success is dependent (often) on the extent to which we can focus our attention analytically. In competition with others, we dare not miss the next move. Our bodies, of course, are active participants in this process. The muscles around our eyes tighten, our foreheads wrinkle, our lips, tongue, and throat quiver as we "chatter" on and on to ourselves about the task at hand or the stakes at risk.

To "actively" strive for profound relaxation is to ensure that you will not obtain it. Instead, you must assume a non-striving state of mind. You must concentrate in a passive, non-focused manner. Be casual with respect to the thoughts and sensations that spring into your mind. Troublesome thoughts will intrude but when they do remind yourself that there is plenty of time to think about them later. Allow them to pass through your awareness as you allow your body to move without interruption toward more profound levels of relaxation. The Zen metaphor for this state of mind compares the mind to a lake with thoughts, like geese, flying over. If any should "land", as happens, they will sooner depart if you can not care about them for now, i.e., if witnessed passively.

There is a Chinese word that captures the essence of this passive mode of mental functioning. The word, *wu wei,* translates as "not doing" but literally means *not forcing.*[6] This is the point. You cannot force your way into the passive mode of concentration or into profound relaxation. Such effort is incompatible with the state you are trying to achieve. By cultivating the ability to shift to the "not forcing" state of mind, you free yourself from the fatigue brought on by over-involvement with your own thoughts. This opens the way to profound levels of relaxation.

STUDY GUIDE / REVIEW

Complete each statement by filling in the blank. Return to the text, if necessary, for review as well as to verify the accuracy of your answers.

1. The relaxation script will help you learn how to _____ relax.

2. The script will help you increase your ability to _____ and eliminate unwanted tension.

3. The script contains a series of _____-_____ exercises.

4. Each exercise involves a different set of _____.

5. The first step of every exercise involves _____ a specific muscle or muscle group.

6. In following this instruction you should try to _____ the tension in the specific muscle being exercised.

7. To complete the exercise, you will be instructed to _____ the muscle.

8. Your effort in the second step of each exercise should be to let the exercised muscle become as _____ and limp as possible.

9. This training procedure will help you _____ the presence and absence of tension in that muscle area.

10. Your rate of learning will be a function of how well you are able to _____ focus your attention on the sensations coming from the exercised muscle.

11. The script will ask you to momentarily _____ all other thoughts and take note of the sensations coming from the region being exercised.

12. Success at directing your attention in the prescribed fashion will allow you to sooner recognize the subtle _____ associated with the increase and decrease of tension.

13. These cues will become signposts or markers allowing you to _____ the environment within your skin.

14. The script also involves a backward counting from five to _____.

15. With each count you should allow yourself to sink more deeply into _____.

16. The script ends by instructing you to _____ your fingers and toes.

17. This helps ensure _____.

18. At the end of a relaxation session you should allow yourself a few minutes to _____.

19. The muscles constitute about _____ the weight of the entire body.

20. Where the muscles lead, the rest of the body is likely to _____.

21. To varying degrees we already have the skill we hope to refine; namely, the ability to _____ subtle changes in our level of muscle tension.

22. As worry increases so too does _____ muscle tension.

23. By learning to thoroughly relax the jaws, lips, throat, tongue, eyes, and forehead, you will be learning how to shut off your overactive _____.

24. The shift from the aroused or activated condition of everyday activity to the profoundly relaxed condition produces a number of bodily _____.

25. As you begin to relax you may notice an + increase in saliva, resulting in a frequent need to _____.

26. Unexpected twitches may occur as pockets of trapped tension are _____.

27. A common sensation is that of _____ in the arms and legs.

28. As blood flows to the periphery you are likely to experience the sensation of _____ in your hands, arms, feet and legs.

29. As your muscles relax you may become aware of what seems like an unusual pounding in your _____.

30. You also may notice that your breathing develops a slow and _____ pattern.

31. It is not uncommon to experience _____ or drifting sensations.

32. You may even feel detached from your own _____ as though you were no longer anchored to your trunk and limbs.

33. You may find that your _____ become less organized, that they begin to flow along by themselves.

34. Forgotten _____ may return, only to be followed by a sequence of vivid, though unconnected and fleeting images.

35. Some of the images will absorb your _____ and leave you with the sense of having been a part of the image.

36. On some occasions you may fall _____.

37. The state of mind that facilitates movement into the profoundly relaxed condition is called passive _____.

38. When in this state of mind your respond to thoughts, feelings, and sensations with utter _____.

39. In this state of mind, rather than trying to be in control, you simply let yourself _____.

40. A Chinese word, "wu wei," captures the essence of this state of mind. It means not- _____.

*Be sure that you have completed all statements accurately
before moving on to the exercises.*

EXERCISE C: Developing a Relaxation Schedule

The purpose of Exercise C is to help you commit to a time and place to practice profound relaxation. Committing time for daily practice is an important step, particularly important in the first week of practice since you are trying to learn a new skill and cultivate a new habit.

Select as practice times those periods of the day that are *least* likely to have interruptions. In addition, make yourself as *inaccessible* as possible during the practice period. This may mean turning off your phone, or asking your spouse to manage the children in a distant room.

Lighting should be directed away from your eyes and, if desired, dimmed or shut off completely. Your clothing should be loosened, allowing you to breathe freely (e.g. ties and neck buttons undone, belts and waistbands unhooked, shoes off or untied). Finally, the room selected for relaxation should be a comfortable temperature. Trying to relax in a room that is too hot or too cold will promote sleeping or shivering, respectively.

There are three positions in which to practice profound relaxation:

1) *Lying* with your back against a firm mattress, arms and legs comfortably extended, back straight and head at the same level as the rest of your body.

2) *Reclining* in a lounge chair, feet up, arms placed comfortably on the arms of the chair with head and neck resting against the back of the chair.

3) *Sitting* erect in a straight-back chair, back straight, head erect, arms resting in your lap or on the arms of the chair with both feet flat on the floor.

With the above information in mind, complete a seven-day schedule by following the directions below. When you have completed the directions move to the next exercise.

1) Turn to the first Relaxation Schedule in Appendix B. Write in the date, time, location, and position in the areas provided.

2) In the "Arrangements" column, write brief phrases indicating what arrangements you must make in order to reduce the likelihood of interruptions during the practice session. (See the schedule on the next page.)

3) Repeat these steps as you complete Relaxation Schedules for the next six days. If possible, use Appendix B as a second date book, scheduling other activities around practice times.

4) When you have completed a week of practice, continue to schedule daily practice sessions for another three weeks. A month's worth of practice will go a long way toward developing the ability to deeply relax when desired or needed.

RELAXATION SCHEDULE

Day: _____   Date: _____

	Time	Location	Position	Arrangements
8:00 – 8:30				
8:30 – 9:00				
9:00 – 9:30				
9:30 – 10:00				
10:00 – 10:30				
10:30 – 11:00				
11:00 – 11:30				
11:30 – 12:00				
12:00 – 12:30				
12:30 – 1:00				
1:00 – 1:30				
1:30 – 2:00				
2:00 – 2:30				
2:30 – 3:00				
3:00 – 3:30	√	*Bedroom*	*Sitting*	*1. Turn off lights*
3:30 – 4:00				*2. Turn off phone*
4:00 – 4:30				*3. Ask spouse to keep*
4:30 – 5:00				*kids in a far room*
5:00 – 5:30				*4. Ask spouse to*
5:30 – 6:00				*knock in 40 min.*
6:00 – 6:30				
6:30 – 7:00				
7:00 – 7:30				
7:30 – 8:00				
8:00 – 8:30				
8:30 – 9:00				
9:00 – 9:30				
9:30 – 10:00				

EXERCISE D: Evaluating a Relaxation Session

The purpose of this exercise is to explain the evaluation form that you will use to evaluate each relaxation session. The evaluation of each relaxation session will provide you with one measure of your progress.

The evaluation form, which is to be completed following each practice session, consists of two parts. The first part asks you to review a list of feelings and sensations and to place a checkmark beside those experienced during the session. Column I contains a list of unpleasant or negative feelings while Column II contains feelings and sensations more commonly associated with profound relaxation. At the bottom of Column I is a space for you to specify the factor(s) responsible for any checkmarks in Column I. Be as specific as possible about these factors. In so doing, you may be identifying issues that may require your attention.

The second part of the evaluation form asks you to rate the depth of relaxation obtained *during* the session. A rating scale from 0 to 5 is provided.

Read the directions listed below. When you have completed the Progress Check accompanying this chapter, you will be ready to begin training.

<u>Directions</u>:

1) Evaluation forms are enclosed in Appendix C. Following each relaxation session, complete an evaluation form by first placing a checkmark beside the feelings and sensations experienced during the practice session.

2) Specify, if you can, the factors responsible for checkmarks in Column I.

3) Rate the depth of relaxation obtained during the session in the space provided. (See sample form)

RELAXATION SESSION EVALUATION FORM

During the relaxation session, I experienced the following:

Column I		Column II	
brief feelings of panic		restful alertness	√
anxiety		saliva increase	√
vulnerability		sudden muscle twitches	
frustration or irritability		heaviness in arms	
sadness or depression		heaviness in legs	√
unpleasant thoughts		numbness in arms or legs	√
feeling of being closed in		warmth in arms or legs	
desire to end session	√	warmth all over	√
sexual worries		tingling sensations	
thoughts on commitments	√	heart pounding	√
erratic breathing		awareness of breathing	
tearing from eyes		feelings of detachment	
tightness in throat or chest		physical relaxation	√
cold hands		floating/drifting sensations	
tension in arms or legs		forgotten memories	
feeling of losing control		unusual images	
		fleeting images	
What in my life is responsible for the check marks in Column I?		vivid and static images	
		vivid and moving images	
		feelings of "letting go"	
		mental relaxation	
I was too harsh earlier today when I disciplined my child.		pleasant feelings	
		calmness	
		joy or euphoria	

Using the scale below, I rate the depth of relaxation obtained during the relaxation session at the following level: __4__

    5 – no more relaxed than when I started
    4 – more relaxed than when I started
    3 – relaxed
    2 – very relaxed
    1 – deeply relaxed
    0 – completely and thoroughly relaxed, calm and peaceful (profoundly relaxed)

PROGRESS CHECK

Answer the questions below as accurately as you can. When you have finished, check your answers with those in the answer key—Appendix A.

1. It is important to practice profound relaxation at least _____ a day.

2. The relaxation training script contains a series of _____ - _____ exercises.

3. These exercises will help you recognize the _____ associated with tension increase and tension decrease.

4. Following the exercises each lesson has a backward counting sequence from _____ to _____.

5. With each count you should allow yourself to become more deeply _____.

6. As your body shifts from an activated condition to a profoundly relaxed condition you will experience a number of bodily _____.

7. The state of mind that facilitates your body's shift into the profoundly relaxed condition is called _____ concentration.

8. When in this state of mind you respond to thoughts, feelings and sensations with utter _____.

9. You should select as daily practice times those periods that are _____ likely to have interruptions.

10. The three positions for practicing profound relaxation are _____, _____, and _____.

11. During the practice session lighting should be directed away from your _____.

12. Clothing should be loosened, allowing you to _____ freely.

13. It is important that you cultivate the _____ of daily practice.

14. Following each practice session you should complete the Relaxation Session _____ Form.

15. On that form you are asked to identify any factors responsible for checkmarks placed in Column _____.

16. In so doing you will be identifying very possibly the _____ with which you must deal if you are to relax whenever you choose.

Check your answers against those listed in the Answer Key.

With the completion of Chapter II you are ready to begin relaxation training. Go to Appendix B and follow the instructions for completing the relaxation tape or CD. Then turn to Appendix C and begin your daily practice on the day and time selected.

Chapter III

Differential Relaxation: Definition & Rationale

The purpose of this chapter is to discuss differential relaxation,[1] the relaxation that is available to you as you go about the requirements of everyday life. There are three practices that promote differential relaxation: First, the practice of quieting the chatter-filled mind so as not to mask the body's subtle processes with excessive "noise"; second, the practice of "scanning" the body for signs of tension; and third, the practice of deliberate living (the focusing of attention and effort on one task at a time). When the events of everyday life flood you with tension and anxiety, the practice of any one of these can help you find your way back to the differentially relaxed mode. To see how this is so, we begin by considering your primary ally in your effort to remain relaxed though active, the body itself.

THE WISDOM OF THE BODY

The human body is comprised of circuitry upon which its various parts send signals concerning their status to the brain. The individual who is sensitive to these signals, who is capable of detecting them, is in a position to make adjustments that help ensure health and wellbeing. There is wisdom in this arrangement because the body is providing information on its wellbeing to the only person who can take immediate corrective action.

Consider, for example, the migraine sufferer who experiences an increase in muscular tension (perhaps even a mild tension headache) hours before the onset of the migraine. The increase in muscular tension is the migraine sufferer's signal to relax, perhaps change course, let go even by degree of the full-steam ahead approach to whatever he or she is doing. If a change in course is done soon enough, the migraine might be avoided. Similarly, consider the person who continues to drink despite a slight sense of disorientation only to be overtaken by nausea and vomiting a few hours later. Or, the millions of smokers who continue to smoke despite the gagging, eye-burning experience of their first few cigarettes. Our bodies are continuously sending us signals concerning the advisability of our ongoing activity. And one of these signals, the "all is not well" signal,[2] as Sidney Jourard calls it, is designed to help us identify activities causing us discomfort and *dis-ease*. By attending to the "all is not well" signal we are in a position to know when adjustments in behavior are needed if health and wellbeing are to be maintained.

The "all is not well" signal, which can come from any part of the body—muscles, organs, joints, the nervous system generally, announces that something may be "off". There is a slight but detectable drop in the sense of wellbeing, a feeling perhaps of disorientation, an unusual degree of stress, tension or anxiety. The purpose of this distress signal is to alert you to a condition or situation that may be deleterious. *Your task, then, is to look into it, into what's going on.* You may need to see a doctor. That's a possibility. Or you may need to look into your lifestyle, your relationships, your choices. That, too, is a possibility. At base, the "all is not well" signal asks you to *take note of what you are doing (and what you've been doing); it asks you to evaluate the suitability of ongoing activity.*[3] Had the migraine sufferer evaluated sooner the "suitability" of his tension-inducing activity (a heated argument with his spouse, for example), he might have switched to a new activity (a new topic, another approach) and thereby made less likely the migraine. The "all is not well" signal helps us wake up to what might be a threat to our wellbeing and perhaps wake up, as well, to what we, ourselves, may be doing to threaten our wellbeing. It is by constructively responding to the "all is not well" signal that an additional degree of self-direction is introduced into our lives.

Yet, as Sidney Jourard points out in his book, *The Transparent Self,* very few of us attend with any regularity to the "all is not well" signal, at least as it first arises. This is due, in part, to the low or "weak intensity" of the signal in its initial phase. The result is that we attend only to the latter phase, the highly assertive phase that takes the form of headache, nausea, generalized anxiety, high blood pressure, dizziness, depression. There are at least two reasons for this: first, we have a difficult time detecting *any* low intensity signal against the background of "noise" produced by our chattering minds, and second, we too infrequently look to our bodies for guidance on matters of health and wellbeing.

Thus, there are two habits—if they have become habits—that need to be broken if we are to utilize the wisdom of the body. The first is our habit of engaging in continuous self-chatter, that constant stream of useless worry and internal gossip; and the second is our habit of only looking outside the body (rather than inside) for clues to health and wellbeing. Instead, in both cases we need to do the opposite. We need to quiet the mind to the extent we can, and thereby reduce the "noise"; and we need to shift our attention (part of it) in the direction of the body, so we can detect the "all is not well" signal when it first occurs. These are helpful steps—new habits, perhaps—that if practiced regularly begin to allow the body its rightful say in how we choose to treat it.

THE NOISE MACHINE[4]

Robert de Ropp, biochemist and author of *The Master Game,* compares the mind to "a badly designed radio, generating so much noise (using this term in the electronic sense) that every incoming message is distorted."[5]

Consider the activity of your own mind. If you are like most of us, you are constantly churning out an enormous flow of words. It seems we never tire of talking to ourselves. We reason, compare, rationalize, gossip, worry, fantasize, all without the encouragement of an audience (other than the one we provide ourselves). We are literally besieged by our own thoughts; confronted, as it were, by a ceaseless "flood of inner conversations, arguments, schemes and aimless chatter."[6] This is the "noise" that fills our minds, obscuring and distorting incoming messages.

The "incoming" messages come from within the body as well as from the sights, sounds, smells, tastes, and textures of the outer world. We lose touch with our bodies and with the outer world because the incoming messages are masked by our "noisy chatter". As a result, it is only the assertive or particularly vivid or painful message that breaks through. Anything less assertive is masked by the constant chatter.

The problem is compounded when we consider how captured we sometimes are by our own thoughts. So interesting are the weavings of the mind that we often surrender our undivided attention to them, submitting the body to a reality of our own making. Consider, for example, the physical arousal that results from a sexual fantasy, or the anger that emerges while ruminating over yesterday's heated argument with a co-worker. Both are examples of how our minds take over our bodies and how we experience the feelings appropriate to what is imagined.

The out-of-control chattering mind (if that is what one is dealing with, and most of us are from time to time) obscures and distorts incoming signals, whether from the body or external environment, adding difficulty to our effort to detect, discern, and navigate. Through endless obsessive worry, for example, we find we are less available for the tasks to which we say we are committed. The thinking mind—our great ally and key to our understanding and our creativity—can come to operate wildly and function at odds with our sense of purpose. There are three strategies, generally speaking, for reining it in.[7]

Muscle Control. The muscles of the face and throat are intimately involved in speech, even the covert speech we call thinking. Edmund Jacobson, the developer of Progressive Relaxation, reports that his patients cease talking to themselves when their facial muscle tension drops below a certain level. By observing your facial musculature you can gain a keen appreciation of its involvement in covert speech. You may notice, for example, that your forehead wrinkles as you ponder a problem; that your eyes narrow and strain as you "see" imaginary events; that your tongue contorts as you converse with a figment. One way of reducing the noise in your over-active mind is to *relax away these tensions.* In practice, this means smoothing out the forehead, allowing the tongue to swell and remain still, loosening the jaw, freeing the eyes from the requirement to see imaginary sights, relaxing fully the lips and throat; in sum, allowing the facial musculature to come down to no more than the moment requires. This, incidentally, will not eliminate facial expression but will allow for a natural, more spontaneous expression. You're less distracted, less distant from the moment wherein interpersonal exchanges are occurring.

Breath Control. A second strategy for quieting the chattering mind is breath control. When you are absorbed with your own thoughts your breathing is likely to be irregular. Upon close inspection you may find that you are breathing in time with the cadence of your inner speech, taking quick breaths to supply the force needed to continue your imaginary discussion. You also may notice that the content of your thoughts influences your breathing. Reliving an anxiety-provoking incident or fantasizing about how you will meet tomorrow's demands can accelerate your breathing. To counter, you need to practice smooth and rhythmic breathing. For several minutes each day you may find it useful to breathe in an uninterrupted pattern, with smooth inhalations and exhalations. When so doing, focus only on your breathing and return to it whenever you become aware that your thoughts have pulled you away. This is an important skill to develop and you should take advantage of your many opportunities to practice it: waiting in line, walking, sitting, riding in a car, any place where you have a history of "working yourself up."

Attention Control. Finally, focusing your attention on events taking place outside your own head is a useful technique for quieting the mind's chatter. For most of us, our own thoughts are so compelling that they can gradually capture our full attention; and few factors encourage verbosity like a captive audience. Yet few factors discourage verbosity like the absence or inattention of an audience. Therefore, you may need to practice directing your attention away from your own thoughts, focusing your attention instead on the events of your surrounding environment or on the events occurring in your body. Indeed, for a variety of reasons, you should practice directing your attention in a *deliberate* fashion, deciding to focus first here and then there rather than having your attention pulled about like "a feather for every wind that blows."[8] When obsessive thoughts and inner conversations again seize your attention, it is your deliberate decision to focus your attention elsewhere that will free it. By continuing to return your focus to your immediate environment *and to what you are doing right now,* you will be loosening the noisemaker's hold over your attention.

In actual practice, all three strategies are combined in an effort to quiet the mind. Throughout each waking hour you should look for opportunities to silence the noise by cultivating habits that successfully compete with it. Those habits include a relaxed facial musculature, a smooth and rhythmic breathing pattern, a deliberate focusing of attention on the events transpiring in muscle, organ, and external world. This is not to say that you should stop thinking. On the contrary, it is the quiet mind that thinks most clearly and from whose depths insights emerge. It is the noise of the undisciplined mind that gums up our thinking, both directly, by making it difficult to stay with a single line of thought, and indirectly, by obscuring the clarity of perception so essential to clear thought.

SCANNING THE INNER ENVIRONMENT

Quieting the noise machine is not the only habit we need to cultivate if we are to utilize the wisdom of the body. We also need to acquire the habit of scanning the body for its low intensity distress signals. The purpose of this scanning is to ensure that we don't miss any "clues" to healthful patterns of behavior. By bringing the low intensity distress signal into our field of attention we provide the body with its proper representation in all decisions concerning its treatment. This promotes self-direction and is one sense in which there is truth to the adage that one should "look inside for the clues to health and happiness."

Most of us, however, have the tendency to look outside to the rules of custom and upbringing. How often have you continued to eat because there was food on your plate even though your body "told" you to stop? How often have you continued to sit in front of the television even though your body was restless and "calling" for exercise? From a very early age we are urged to conform to the dictates of external authority, (i.e., parents, teachers, peers). This is useful, of course, because it offers protection and guidance. But this arrangement was to continue only until we could make more of our own decisions, until we could behave responsibly with respect to the issues that influence us. Once that point was reached, the rules of parents and community were to serve only as guidelines for what is *likely* to be health-promoting but may *not* be given the unique set of circumstances in which we find ourselves. Part of the information relevant to making a decision about what behavior promotes our wellbeing comes from within the body. Our habit of looking outside, to external authorities, can prevent us from obtaining guidance from within.

There are many useful techniques for reminding us to scan for the low intensity "all is not well" signal. Thomas Budzynski, a biofeedback researcher and clinician, encourages his clients to wear "a sliver of brightly colored tape on their wrist watch dial."[9] Each time they look at their watch they are reminded to "scan around for tension spots."[10] Relaxation therapists often encourage their clients to scan for inappropriate tension prior to going through a doorway. In this way, they provide their clients with frequent reminders to scan for tension, . . . in the same way that the Jewish household provides itself with a frequent opportunity for personal reflection by placing a mezuzah next to each doorway. Similarly, anything frequently encountered can serve to prompt an inward glance. Diaries, hourly checklists, and other such devices may be useful in this regard. They help remind us that simply quieting the noisemaker is not enough. We also must scan the body for its low intensity distress signal. By so doing, we provide ourselves with a useful source of wisdom and guidance.

DIFFERENTIAL RELAXATION

Differential relaxation means *exerting only the amount of tension and energy required to perform a given act properly.*[11] This is not how most of us meet the demands of everyday life. Consider the simple though at times perilous act of driving a car. All that is required when driving is the use of the arms, sometimes both legs, erect posture, an alert mind. Even so, many of us find that we also tense our upper backs, our stomachs, our faces. At stoplights we clinch the steering wheel, tap our feet, and roar with self-chatter. All of this excess tension competes with our ability to assess the routine demands of driving. Errors in judgment are more likely under these conditions and these errors—slight though they may be—further complicate and endanger the situation. This can become a dangerous spiral and it is not unlike the way we face many of life's simple demands. Our approach—not always but on occasion—is to put more energy into the situation than is required, hoping we can end it, or change it in the shortest and most painless fashion. Instead, we sometimes make it worse.

An Indian philosopher and teacher, Shree Rajneesh, provided in one of his books a useful distinction for clarifying the meaning of differential relaxation.[12] The distinction is between "action" and "activity." Action is a response to a specific demand, a demand from the body or the external environment or one's own creative callings. Such action is proper and appropriate. Activity, on the other hand, is when there is no demand, no legitimate call to act *and you act anyway*. Rajneesh uses the example of eating to illustrate the distinction. Action is when you eat because you are hungry. Eating continues only until the hunger is satisfied. Activity is when there is no hunger and "still you go on eating."[13] This sort of eating, this activity, is driven by "inner restlessness." Thus, "activity is when the response has no relevance" and according to Rajneesh, "ninety percent of our energy is wasted in 'activity.' And because of this, when the moment for action comes, we don't have any energy."[14] Differential relaxation is the same as "action," as Rejneesh has defined it, and is characterized by an absence of "activity." To quote again from Rajneesh, "Relaxation comes to you when there is no urge for activity; the energy is at home, not moving anywhere. If a certain situation arises you will act, that's all, but you are not finding some excuse to act. You are at ease with yourself."[15]

It now should be clear how a noise-free mind and the habit of scanning the inner environment interact to promote the practice of differential relaxation. As unnecessary "noise" is reduced, clarity increases. The low intensity "all is not well" signal is more likely to be detected. Both body and mind can have their rightful say in how much energy you choose to put into your ongoing activity. To these two factors a third must be added. This third factor addresses the problem implicit in the over-committed, highly complicated lifestyle where the individual is met (or so it seems) with several legitimate demands at once. The result can be paralysis. The individual finds him or herself caught between equally deserving issues while never taking steps to properly address any of them. This leads to wasted time and energy, and often, to self-recrimination and thus, to the loss of the differentially relaxed mode. The antidote for this is the practice of deliberate living or, as Robert de Ropp has called it, "intentional doing."[16]

DELIBERATE LIVING

"Intentional doing" means performing a deliberately selected act through to its proper completion without being pulled into unintended activities. Its practice requires that you "know what you are doing and why."[17] You may have decided that now is the time to read the newspaper, or brush your teeth, or write an overdue letter; the act itself may not appear significant but the decision to perform the act is and should not be compromised readily. The challenge emerges as soon as you set out to complete the act. As you step from one room to another, indeed, as you turn your head in a new direction, you are confronted with a barrage of new stimuli, each pulling on your attention, each calling you to other activities. The confusion is compounded by the flow of still more stimuli as you find you are, in T. S. Eliot's words, "distracted from distraction by distraction."[18] However, as long as your decision is firmly grounded in the knowledge of what you are doing and why, and so long as you are not met with a real (as opposed to imagined) emergency, you should continue as you intended. By so doing you will begin to imbue your decision-making with the power of follow-through.

De Ropp illustrates the weakness of our follow-through by pointing to the man who, while gardening in the hot sun, decides he must go inside and get his hat.

"... suppose as he enters the house he notices dust on the furniture, finds fault with his spouse on this score and gets into an argument: "Why do I live in a pigsty?" The hat is forgotten. Instead, he is quarreling with his spouse. Later, when he has stopped quarreling, he cannot remember why he came into the house in the first place. He must go back into the garden, where the impact of the hot sun on his bald pate reminds him of his first intention—to get his hat. So he must make a second trip into the house to perform what he had intended to do in the first place."[19]

Not allowing two or more seemingly legitimate demands to compete successfully for your attention, as the man did in the above example, is the essence of deliberate living. This does not mean that legitimate demands are ignored. On the contrary, it means that each demand is potentially legitimate and therefore deserving of your full attention. Thus, the strategy implicit in the practice of deliberate living requires that you respond to one demand at a time and that you stay with it until you have completed what you intended to accomplish. If emergencies arise, you attend to them, dropping all else and focusing with a well-practiced deliberateness that gets the job done. But you are not fabricating emergencies (or yielding to distractions) and that's the difference.

De Ropp offers two key suggestions for the practice of deliberate living. He writes that in all tasks, big and small, you should first *"know what you are doing and why."*[20] This involves specifying clearly what you are choosing to do, providing yourself a reason for doing it, and giving yourself a limited amount of time in which to complete it (or to do what you intended). In short, it means preparing yourself for the task by owning up to your choice, taking responsibility for whatever you have chosen to do. When "activity" emerges, that is, when you lose the differentially relaxed mode, you should stop and "return to the starting point."[21] This is de Ropp's second suggestion; namely, that distractions of whatever form are your signal to stop and "redefine your intention."[22] Having regained your sense of direction, you can again set out to accomplish what you intend. By continuing to practice these simple suggestions, according to de Ropp, you gain greater self-control, and in the process eliminate the "activity" that results from the absence of purpose and intention.

SUMMARY

The focus of this chapter has been on the factors crucial to the practice of differential relaxation. Cultivating a quiet mind, to the extent possible, and scanning the body for its low intensity "all is not well" signal are crucial steps in the effort to utilize the wisdom of the body. And deliberate living, the performing of a deliberately selected act through to the completion of what is intended, helps us maintain the differentially relaxation mode by making us less vulnerable to the anxiety and tension that results from our failure to complete one task when confronted with many.

STUDY GUIDE / REVIEW

Complete each statement by filling in the blank. Return to the text for review as well as to verify the accuracy of your answers.

1. The focus of this chapter is on _____ relaxation.

2. This is the relaxation for everyday _____.

3. Name the three practices supportive of this mode of relaxation.

   1) _____

   2) _____

   3) _____

4. In the course of evolutionary adaptation, the body has found advantage in evolving a circuitry upon which its various parts send _____ concerning their status to the brain.

5. The individual who is sensitive to the body's messages can make the adjustments in _____ that help insure health and wellbeing.

6. One of the signals that the body occasionally sends us is called the "_____" signal.

7. This is a very important signal because it helps us _____ the activities that may be causing us to suffer discomfort and disease.

8. This signal can come from any part of the _____.

9. The message that this signal conveys is that it is time to _____ the suitability of your current activity.

10. By attending and constructive responding to this signal, we introduce an additional degree of _____-_____ into our lives.

11. Unfortunately, most of us do not attend with any regularity to this signal, at least as it first _____.

12. One of the reasons we have a difficult time detecting this signal is because of the _____ produced by our chattering minds.

13. Another reason is that we too infrequently look to our _____ for guidance on matters of health.

14. In order to utilize the wisdom implicit in this signal, you must quiet your _____ mind,

15. as well as learn to shift your _____ in the direction of your body.

16. By so doing, you will be allowing your body its rightful say in how you choose to _____ it.

17. We fail to detect the body's low intensity distress signals because of our noisy minds. As a consequence, only the assertive or _____ message breaks through to us.

18. Another way in which our noisy minds exert an undesirable influence over us is by pulling our _____ away from the activity to which we have committed ourselves.

19. One way to quiet the overactive mind is to relax the _____ of the face and throat.

20. A second strategy to employ against the noise-filled mind is _____ control.

21. This involves the practice of smooth and rhythmic _____ .

22. Finally, focusing your attention on the immediate events taking place outside your own _____ is useful in quieting the mind.

23. Differential relaxation means exerting only the amount of tension and energy required to perform a given act _____.

24. A useful distinction for clarifying the meaning of this mode of relaxation is between action and _____.

25. An additional factor related to this mode of relaxation is the practice of _____ living.

26. Intentional doing, to use de Ropp's phrase, means performing an intentionally selected act through to its proper completion without being pulled into _____ activities.

27. Its practice requires that you know what you are doing and _____.

28. The act you select to perform at any given moment may not appear to be important but the _____ to perform the act is important.

29. By not compromising your intent you will be imbuing your decisions with the power of _____-_____.

30. Deliberate living or intentional doing requires that you respond to _____ demand at a time.

31. Distractions or forgetfulness are your signals to stop and redefine your _____.

Be sure that you have completed all statements accurately before moving on to the exercises.

EXERCISE E: Proper Bodily Posture

Standing, walking, sitting and lying were once called *the four dignities of man*.[23] Since time immemorial they have served as fundamental indicators of a person's self-esteem. This exercise outlines the basics of proper bodily posture.

It is true that postures vary, that by middle age, if not before, many of us have assumed postural habits that vary from those most suited to the body's structure. (And it is also true that disease—arthritis, for example—can dramatically affect one's posture.) Common such habits include drooping shoulders/drooping head, turned-out toes, turned-in or pigeon toes, rounded back, swayback, stiffness from the shoulders to the legs, all of which lead to a loss of rhythm in the simplest movements. Yet, it is also true that proper posture often can be recovered and, indeed, made habitual with the aid of practice, heightened self-awareness and, in some cases, exercises designed to strengthen the muscles of the trunk and abdomen.[24]

There are three reasons for maintaining proper posture.[25] First, proper posture ensures the bodily alignment that affords maximal mechanical efficiency, thereby making available the potential of each muscle. Second, proper posture provides freedom from unnecessary strain since it avoids a disproportionate reliance on one muscle group or bodily region at the expense of another. Common strains resulting from poor posture "occur in the major weight-bearing joints, such as those of the lower back, the hips, knees, ankles and arches."[26] Such strains can ultimately lead to arthritic changes.[27] And finally, proper bodily posture provides a minimum of interference with organic function; digestive and respiratory processes remain free of unnatural pressures from adjacent organs or muscles.

For our purposes it should be added that proper posture goes hand in hand with the practice of differential relaxation. Improper posture leads prematurely to fatigue since some muscles are required to work excessively while others remain uninvolved. This spells tension, the "all is not well" signal, and sooner than later, the loss of the differentially relaxed mode. This is the reason that proper posture is so necessary for relaxation. Without it you are in the paradoxical position of trying to relax away tensions that are being produced continuously by a body in poor alignment.

Review your own posture by comparing it to the posture that results from following the instructions provided below. A full-length mirror is useful for this purpose. Remember that body types vary and that your primary goal is a posture that offers balance plus the proper alignment of body segments. If proper posture proves difficult, seek out one of the many books detailing exercises designed to strengthen the muscles needed for such posture.

Standing:[28]

1. The total body weight is centered squarely above both feet or else is very slightly forward, but never backward.

2. The major weight-bearing segments of the body (the lower extremities, pelvis, trunk and head) are aligned in a single straight line, either vertical or slanting very slightly forward from the ankles.

3. The pelvis is centered squarely above the feet and beneath the trunk.

4. The chest is lightly lifted but the elevation is not forced.

5. The head is erect with the profile vertical and the chin level.

6. The feet point forward or slightly outward.

7. The ankles, as seen from the front or back, are straight.

8. The total posture is maintained without evidence of strain or tension.

9. Refine your standing posture with the following: " . . . stand with feet parallel, a foot's breadth apart. Swing your body slowly backward and forward from the ankle joints like a pendulum. The swing must not be so great that you raise the heels or grip with the toes. Swing so slowly that you have time to note what happens in your body. Do you feel the shift between tension and relaxation? Do you feel that the tension is maximal at the extreme backward point of oscillation, decreases toward the middle until it reaches a minimum, from where it again increases until the opposite extreme limit?"[29]

Walking:

1. Proper walking posture incorporates the balanced standing posture just discussed. From the standing position you begin by putting your weight forward. When you do so you will notice that your foot moves forward in a spontaneous effort to restore balance. The process proceeds as "the back foot takes off with all toes, thereby pushing the body forward; the leg is then swung loosely forward with both ankle and knee joints bent; with the heel down first, but immediately the weight is carried over to the front of the foot. The foot that is now at the rear then takes off with all toes, and so forth."[30]

2. The toes point forward rather than to the side where they would be incapable of pushing the body forward.[31]

3. "The hips should move forward and back, rather than side to side, lifting slightly at the beginning of each stride . . ."[32]

4. The shoulders "also take part in the movement. It is the rotary movements of the shoulders that make the arms swing. The arms do not use any force to swing; on the contrary, it takes muscular force (held tension) to prevent them from swinging."[33]

5. Refine your walking posture by imagining "that a force is pulling you upward and at the same time another force is pulling you forward from the breastbone.[34] Continue until you have established a "forward and up" posture while walking.[35]

Sitting:

1. Proper sitting posture involves an erect upper body with the chest slightly lifted, and head and back aligned in a straight line, either vertical or slanting slightly forward.

2. "The buttocks should be the hindmost part of the body . . . not, as with most people, the shoulder blades."[36]

3. The hips should be pushed to the back of the chair and your feet placed flat on the floor, your thighs parallel to the floor. Obviously, the selection of a chair to sit in is crucial. Those that deny support for your lower back, cut off circulation at the knees, or force the thighs to assume an unnatural slant should be avoided.[37]

4. Refine your sitting posture by placing your hands on your knees and making "a slow rocking movement forward and backward, moving the hips only and maintaining the stable position of the back (neither arching nor curving it). Try in this way to find your position of balance... Be sure that you are creating no undue tension in the legs, lower pelvis, buttocks, back, shoulders, arms or neck."[38] The point of balance identifies the correct sitting posture.

<u>Lying</u>:

Rather than defining a specific posture, this section focuses on the bed in which you spend up to one-third of your time.[39]

1. The foundation of the bed must be completely unyielding and the mattress firm. In case of a lean person with pronounced curves (broad hips, narrow waistline) who sleeps on the side, a spring or polyester mattress will be suitable... A well-padded person, or one without marked curves, can with advantage sleep on a horsehair mattress placed on a wooden bed bottom. The pillow should be small, just under the head and neck (the shoulders should be free of the pillow).[40]

Standing, walking, sitting and lying, the four dignities of man and woman, are intimately linked to differential relaxation. Check yourself daily on these four "dignities," become aware of them. Correct your slouching and exercise/strengthen your muscles, as needed. The four dignities constitute one reflection of the esteem with which you hold yourself. Deportment, it might be said, begins with them.

EXERCISE F: Building the Will

The will is central to the notion of deliberate living. Without it, there is no follow-through, no capacity to do as one intends. The problem is that the will is like a muscle, it must be exercised or it becomes weak, even lifeless. When in this state it must be brought back, nurtured into the robustness that is needed. *But how?* How is one to bring back a will gone flat?

This exercise suggests one way. It asks you to assume the strategy of the long distance runner who starts out slowly and only gradually increases the distance he will run. With this strategy, the runner avoids strain while building the stamina that brings the longer distances within range. To ask too much too soon is to invite failure and with it, a loss of your "willingness" to proceed. So, the strategy suggested here is one of *gradualism,* a slow build-up to a strengthened and robust will.

In specific terms, this exercise asks you to try on some new activities, new tasks or challenges for a day or a week, and to complete them. Not because there is any virtue in the tasks themselves but because by completing them you strengthen your capacity to do as you intend. These tasks are called *mini-challenges,* "mini" because they are modest in size.

There are two important characteristics to consider when selecting a mini-challenge. First, the mini-challenge should represent a break with your normal routine and second, it should fall into the "I could if I had to" category.

The "normal routine" is sometimes a culprit. While it may afford sufficient time for the day-to-day demands of job and family, it also can squeeze out time devoted to anything else (e.g., "I haven't picked up a tennis racket in months," "We haven't had our own garden in years," "I just don't keep up like I used to."). You are accomplishing what you need to accomplish, or so it seems, and doing so without much strain but something is sneaking up on you. It is your "robot-self," your habit-governed self, accompanied by an unexercised will. By definition, mini-challenges fall outside the normal routine.

The second consideration in selecting a mini-challenge is that you should feel that you are capable of doing it; it should fall into the "I could if I had to" category. Mini-challenges exist just outside the boundary of recent action but within the boundary of presumed capability, into that thin grey area the outer edge of which is defined by what we say we can do and the inner edge by what we, in fact, do. The problem for many of us is that we never find a sufficiently strong excuse for exploring the region of presumed capability. The result is that we become less and less accurate about what we can and can't do—we evolve into talkers rather than doers, excuse makers, old athletes sitting around saying, "If we just got in shape, we'd show those kids." Mini-challenges are a test, an opportunity to prove that you can do as you say. They lead to greater self-knowledge and with success, greater willpower, as well.

When deciding to take on a mini-challenge, begin by saying "I have decided to . . ." naming then the mini-challenge. Say it aloud—to a friend, if necessary—so there is no doubt about your intent. The purpose of this statement is to emphasize who is responsible for the undertaking. You mustn't leave room for an alibi. Either you do it or you don't. Your goal is to make your intent binding and you can't begin to reach that goal if you do not clearly know your intent.

This, then, serves as an introduction to this exercise. What follows is a list of potential mini-challenges. They will qualify as mini-challenges for you if they fall outside your normal routine and into the "I could if I had to" category. If none of these items meets this criterion, then invent your own. Remember: Take on those mini-challenges you feel confident about completing. With success, your willpower will increase, i.e., the follow-through required to face and perhaps overcome major challenges.

> <u>Instructions</u>: *Review the list that follows and put a checkmark next to those items that constitute a mini-challenge for you. If none qualify, then create your own. Then commit yourself to doing one mini-challenge a week for four weeks (or three weeks, or two weeks). Circle those items. At the end of that time, see if you can detect any increase in your sense of willpower, and in your sense of possibility.*

POTENTIAL MINI-CHALLENGES

— Plant a tree
— Fast for 24 hours (drink lots of water)
— Get up one hour earlier for one week
— Work a crossword puzzle
— Give up junk food for one week
— Spend one day completely alone, preferably in the out-of-doors
— Construct a day's schedule—from morning to night—and follow it
— Spend a day without anything scheduled
— Go horseback riding
— Go hang-gliding
— Make a kite
— Give up cigarettes for one week
— Write a short story
— Go through your clothes and get rid of those you never wear
— Organize your kitchen so as to make cooking and cleanup easier
— Paint a picture
— Keep a diary of your important thoughts and feelings for one week
— Live for a week on one-fifth less money (Is that possible?)
— Refuse to worry about any problems for an entire day (Is that possible?)
— Remain silent for 24 hours
— Exercise daily for one week
— Get up at the same hour and go to bed at the same hour for one week
— Vary your sleep and awakening times each day for a week
— Spend a day doing favors/making gifts for friends
— Mend and repair all (or some) of your clothes
— Spend a day figuring out what you would like your children to know
— Don't complain about anything for an entire day
— Spend a day with your children explaining to them what you believe they should know
— Walk rather than drive for one week to all locales within one mile of your home
— Spend a day/week getting everything (most things, one thing) in your house working
— Introduce yourself to people you would like to know
— Volunteer at a homeless shelter
— Read thirty minutes each day for a week on a topic that you've ignored for too long
— Spend a day catching up on correspondence
— Spend a week organizing the closets in your house
— Construct a budget and stick to it—without exception—for one week
— Attend to tasks as soon as they present themselves for an entire day
— Remain unperturbed for an entire day
— Give up meat for one week
— Give up alcohol for one week
— Do one new activity a week for four weeks
— Speak with an Italian accent for an entire day

Others?

_____

_____

_____

PROGRESS CHECK

Answer the questions below as accurately as you can. When you have finished, check your answers with those supplied in the answer key - Appendix A.

1. The three practices supportive of differential relaxation are:

    1) _____

    2) _____

    3) _____

2. Differential relaxation means exerting only the amount of tension and energy required to perform a given act _____.

3. One of the keys to arriving at the differentially relaxed mode of conduct is _____ living.

4. Intentional doing means performing a deliberately selected act through to its proper completion without being pulled into _____ activities.

5. This means that you should respond to _____ demand at a time.

6. Also central to the practice of differential relaxation is proper bodily _____.

7. One of the reasons that this is so important is that it ensures the bodily alignment that affords maximal _____ efficiency, thereby making available the potential of each muscle.

8. A second reason is that it provides freedom from _____ since it avoids a disproportionate reliance on one muscle group or bodily region at the expense of another.

9. Finally, it is important because it ensures a minimum of interference with _____ function; digestive and respiratory processes among others remaining free of unnatural pressures from adjacent organs and muscles.

10. Without proper posture you are in the paradoxical position of trying to relax away tensions that are being continuously _____ by a body in poor alignment.

11. Persistence, follow-through, will-power: these are the keys to _____ living.

12. One way of increasing your will-power is by taking on new activities called _____ - _____.

13. In selecting these activities you should make sure that they fall outside your _____ routine.

14. These activities should also fall beyond the boundary of recent action but within the boundary of presumed capability, into the "_____" category.

15. Finally, when you have selected one of those activities, you should begin by saying "I have _____ ____ naming then the task so as to understand and clearly state your own intent.

16. As your power to live deliberately increases so too, perhaps, does your ability to face and successfully overcome your _____ challenges.

Check your answers against those listed in the Answer Key.

CHAPTER IV

Identifying Anxiety-Inducing Factors

The last chapter concluded with a discussion of mini-challenges, those tasks through which you build the power of follow-through. In this chapter, we focus on your major challenges; those issues that stand between you and the differentially relaxed mode. Put another way, it is in this chapter that we focus on your curriculum; those factors that may need to be addressed if you are to find yourself functioning more often in the differentially relaxed mode. For convenience, these factors are divided into three categories: the situational, the social, and the personal.[1] Later, in the exercises, you will have the opportunity to identify the specific anxiety-inducing factors that may be operating in your life.

SITUATIONAL FACTORS

Situational factors are those factors that can cause the situations in which you find yourself (your workplace, for example) to be stressful. The situational factors discussed below are "sudden and unexpected change," "the blockage of goal-directed behavior," "time performance pressure," "the risk or tedium of certain work," and finally, "the lack of fairness in such areas as job promotion." Review the various situations in which you operate in the light of these factors. Any one of them, if carried to an extreme, can cause health and wellness to suffer.

Sudden and unexpected change. In *Man Adapting,* Rene DuBos quotes Hippocrates who wrote, "It is changes that are chiefly responsible for disease, especially the greatest changes, the violent alterations both in the seasons and in other things. But the seasons which come on gradually are the safest, as are gradual changes of regimen and temperature."[2] Today, in our fast paced world, we seem to have lost contact with the wisdom that calls for gradual change. We have learned that nothing is so ulcer inducing as is the sudden and unexpected change wrought in what was previously thought to be a straightforward and predictable activity. This is particularly true if the change is punitive. Consider, for example, how unnerving it is when your supervisor, having failed to meet his monthly quota, criticizes your job performance, the same performance that on the previous day had been acceptable. Or, how frustrated you feel when your car breaks down just as you are leaving town for a relaxing weekend. This frustration turns to anger when your landlord unexpectedly raises your rent, or you learn that you are next in line to be laid off at the plant. Surprises such as these teach your stomach as well as your analytic mind the health-destroying properties of a situation full of sudden and unexpected change. If you are surprised too often, and the surprises are too frequently unpleasant, you may come to believe (perhaps rightly) that within that situation there is no refuge, no place or time during which you are safe from such surprises. The result can be a constant bracing, a hyper-alertness, with every muscle and gland involved in maintaining a readiness for the next "violent alteration." Of course, that alteration may never come and even if it does it may not provide an opportunity for you to release your physiological readiness; a situation which, as DuBos points out, "is extremely common in civilized life, often frustrating, and likely to be deleterious."[3]

The blockage of goal-directed behavior. The blockage of goal-directed behavior is another factor that brings stress and anxiety into our lives. Unfortunately, situations characterized by this factor are not rare. In our complex world of forms, specialists, complicated regulations, high prices, and competing interests there seems to be a "catch" to everything. How easy it is to have your spirit bruised, even broken, when time after time you are prevented from reaching your goal by obstacles beyond your control. "If you would have just finished high school," or "checked with personnel," or "been here yesterday"—and so on until you no longer believe your goal possible. An extreme example of this predicament is Joseph K., Kafka's hero in his novel *The Trial*.[4] Joseph K.'s regimented and predictable life is turned inside out by the prospect of a "trial." With every effort to exert control over his own fate, he is frustrated by forces that seem always to be beyond his control. He begins to view his own behavior as meaningless and, inevitably, he loses his appetite for life.

To be in a situation that continues to deny you the experience of relevance leads invariably to pessimism and pessimism leads to an apathetic withdrawal, a retreat from the challenges of life. It doesn't take much, a few blocked attempts to reach your goal(s) and you begin to question your competence. Since nothing you do seems to make any difference, you begin to view yourself as irrelevant. Decisions that were previously handled with ease now require enormous effort. Taking charge seems far too onerous. "Better not to fight it," you hear yourself say, "Better to resign yourself to whatever comes." Anxiety is a by-product of this process, as is self-doubt, with depression a possible outcome.

Time performance pressure. In work related situations[5] where "time is money," the necessities of business bring into play a set of time performance pressures that can increase stress and anxiety. Long hours and heavy workloads intended to meet important deadlines add hassles while squeezing out time previously devoted to family, friends, and recreation. Without renewal, without diversion, the long hours at work fill up with "one damn thing after another." If you have any pressing personal issues (marital disputes, problems with children), you may come to resent the long hours because they compete with what you believe to be a greater priority. Add to this developing scenario the likelihood of less exercise and sleep (even the adjustment of sleep cycles with the rotating work shifts of some industries) and you have a form of occupational stress known to blue and white-collar workers alike.

High risk work. Highly complex work requiring a strict attention to detail can also be stressful, particularly if the consequences for error are severe. The air traffic controller, the surgeon, the iron worker, the miner, the pilot, the accountant, the dentist, to name but a few, experience moments requiring supreme concentration. To be always on guard against the "risks" inherent in such work is draining and many find they are unable to free their mind in time to enjoy the other activities of the day. Often, this results in an all-consuming search for methods that reliably relieve the pressure. And some of the more common methods (e.g., alcohol) sooner or later make things worse.

Highly tedious work. Just as stressful as the job involving risk, however, is the job that is so simple and unchallenging that boredom is inevitable. Assembly line work is a good example. Here otherwise complex tasks are broken down into their most rudimentary steps. The by-product of this arrangement can be a drop in worker satisfaction. It is very difficult to convince someone who is engaged eight hours a day in putting hubcaps on wheels or price tags on canned goods that he or she is involved in meaningful work. He may be adequately paid for his efforts and he may purchase many of life's comforts and this may be enough but if he aspires to something more meaningful, the tedium of his current work will disrupt his equilibrium and his health, mental and/or physical, is likely to suffer.

Lack of fair treatment. Finally, the lack of fair treatment in certain work and social situations is another factor capable of producing tension and anxiety. Unfair job promotion is one example. Those individuals who are under-promoted conclude that job performance is unrelated to promotion. This can lead to a loss of enthusiasm and to a search for excuses not to go "beyond the call of duty." Another example can be found in social situations in which one or two individuals dominate to the exclusion of all others. The lack of "floor time" can be frustrating, embarrassing, even angering for those looking forward to an entertaining exchange among equals. More significant still, is life in a society where entire groups—whether for reasons of race, ethnicity, gender, what have you—are treated unfairly. Unfair treatment at that level and to that degree is truly maddening. It makes you sick: spiritually, psychologically, eventually, physically. The presence of this factor in a group, let alone in society at large represents a significant challenge to anyone attempting to keep their blood pressure within an acceptable range.

SOCIAL FACTORS

Social factors are those factors that influence the interpersonal buffers and support networks that protect us from excessive strain. The social factors discussed below are "social mobility," "deviation from socially sanctioned roles," "the family" or its facsimile, and "isolation." These factors contribute to our sense of isolation and aloneness.

Social mobility. Increasing mobility is one of the social factors interacting with our sense of aloneness. We drop job, friends, and family for a higher paying job in the next city. We relocate aging relatives to nursing homes, children to schools across town, and ourselves up the ladder of success. We don't live where we grew up and we wouldn't think of returning. Times change and we are on the move. We move to the city for employment, to the suburbs for "room to move around", and to the country for tranquility. And, above all, we commute, turning our lives into constant motion. Yet, each of us remains an individual with basic human needs, needs such as companionship, support, intimacy; needs satisfied with the aid of time and stability. Without nourishing support and intimacy, we lose one of the buffers protecting us from the stress of everyday life, a stress compounded by constant motion.

Deviation from socially sanctioned roles. Another factor contributing to our aloneness, our sense of isolation is society's lack of tolerance for deviations from its prescribed roles. Society expects its adults to be employed and its parents to be married. It views with suspicion the unconventional and expects its citizens to pursue specific roles at specific times throughout their lives. By deviating too sharply from a prescribed role or by occupying two or more distinct roles for which there are incompatible social expectations (mother-unmarried-adolescent in contrast to mother-married-adult[6]) you run the risk of "sticking out," of being too easy to spot. If the rest of society dislikes what it sees, it may exclude you. How it does so can vary from a cold shoulder to harassment and beyond, any one of which will surely test your stability. The ultimate result of this can be a heightened sense of aloneness as your socially unacceptable "uniqueness" becomes too heavy a burden.

The family. Traditionally, it has been the family that has protected and buffered the individual from the stresses of everyday life. When other agencies and support networks deserted the individual, the family was there to supply "essential nourishment."[7] Michael Novak, in his article entitled, "The Family Out of Favor," writes that it has always been the family (in its various forms) that by itself could make life worth living. Yet, he argues, the necessities of urban industrial life seem to oppose it, decisions favoring political and economic interests over the family. And yet, without some version of the family—some set of relationships in which there is permanence, trust, and unconditional support—the individual is forced to draw on his own resources for fortification and renewal. This can be incredibly taxing, particularly as the irritations of everyday life increase. When caught in this predicament, the individual emerges either fully self-sustaining (a rarity) or not at all, his resources and resistances depleted.

Isolation. The authors of a recent paper reviewing research on life events and illness write, " . . . social isolation has been delineated as a major factor in increased risk of disease. There is now considerable evidence to suggest that those who live alone and are not involved with people or organizations have for this very reason a heightened vulnerability to a variety of chronic diseases."[8]

This comes as no surprise to anyone who has reflected on their own health and how it changes in response to fluctuations in their social network. For example, your children move away and in their wake you experience a nagging depression. This interferes with your sleep, your exercise, your diet. In short order you find that your state of mind has turned your body into a non-resistant host and you catch "whatever it is that's going around." Or, you separate from your spouse and begin your turbulent re-entry into the world of the single person. This process is slow and full of the emotional swings that sap energy and lower resistance. Regardless of how it happens, as soon as your interpersonal and social support system weakens so also does your resistance to disease. Many are able to rebuild and for them the increased susceptibility is temporary. For others, with less time or skill, there remains the "heightened vulnerability to . . . chronic disease" compounded by the dread of facing life and death alone.

PERSONAL FACTORS

Personal factors are viewpoints, attitudes, approaches to life, and/or behaviors that can contribute stress and anxiety to whatever situation we're in. The personal factors discussed below are "blaming others for our morale," "pretending that things should be other than as they are," "bad faith," "over-commitment," "hurry sickness," and "the tendency to live in the past." Each is a good example of how we can threaten our own health by thinking and behaving in unhelpful, perhaps even self-destructive ways.

Blaming others for your morale. It is very difficult to assume responsibility for your morale. Maintaining your morale as you would have it takes commitment, effort, and practice. But to view others as responsible for your morale is to make you dependent on them. This unfairly inhibits others from being themselves when they are around you and makes you emotionally vulnerable when they are. This is a challenging topic. We are, after all, entangled with others, our lives interwoven with family and friends whose wellbeing or lack thereof affects us. We will have ups and downs in response to the condition of loved ones, in response, as well, to the bad luck and disappointments that come our way. Still, our morale is ours to maintain as best we can. It is not for others to determine. Continue with the activities you value, attend to the health of your relationships, proceed ethically in your business and other dealings, these are the age old prescriptions for the maintenance of one's morale, even if things are not going your way. To make yourself dependent on others for your morale is unfair. (After all, others in your life have all they can do dealing with their own morale!) So, to make others responsible is eventually to make yourself a victim. And the victim falls prey sooner or later to self-pity or perhaps rage, indulgences that threaten wellbeing.

Pretending that things should be other than as they are.[9] It is important to remember that everything has a cause, a reason for happening (so say the physicists, so says common sense). The cause may not be apparent (it often isn't) and the result may not be the hoped for result (that often happens as well) but if it happened, it happened because it was made to happen by the events and choices that preceded it. It is, therefore, a waste of energy to believe that something else *should* have happened. This is a tricky line of thought, but imagine, for example, that today is the day that 1) your car is rear-ended; 2) your pay raise doesn't come through; 3) you tip the scale at twenty pounds over your desired weight. "This should not be happening to me," you hear yourself say. (And perhaps, in some sense, it shouldn't be.) Yet, each of these events was led to by preceding events, some of which (but not all) you controlled. An icy street, a bureaucracy full of details and delays, months of overeating, these are the factors that led to today's events. To believe that icy streets should not lead to an accident, or that months of overeating should not lead to overweight is to be irrational. Such thinking can allow you to feel picked-on and opens the door to anger and resentment. As one writer put it, " . . . it isn't what happens that bugs you, it's the things that you say in your head *about* what happens that makes all the machinery get messed up and leads to various varieties of disease."[10] Of related concern is the way in which irrational thinking simply prevents you from changing the troublesome situation (e.g., you are so upset about the issue you cannot face it). The antidote (at least, in part) and only real recourse is to acknowledge the past, to honor it by learning from it, realizing that what will happen in the future is, in large part, up to you and the choices you make now.

Bad Faith. Another common misperception, to carry the discussion one step further, is to assume that we have no choice, "to pretend something is necessary that in fact is voluntary."[11] Peter Berger points out in his book, *Invitation to Sociology: A Humanistic Perspective,* that this is what Jean Paul Satre called *bad faith.* It is, in Berger's terms, a "dishonest evasion of the 'agony of choice'[12] and is, therefore, an attempt to deny personal responsibility for the fate that befalls us. How often have you heard someone say, "I don't have any choice about it," or "I was made or forced to do it." In Dyer's view, this is very likely not true. To believe that it is true is to promote helplessness and ends in resignation. Its by-product is resentment and regret. Carried to an extreme, the practice of bad faith represents an abandonment of personal responsibility, a refusal to be accountable either to ourselves or to others. It is a view that effectively eliminates the person with the most to lose from decisions concerning his or her wellbeing. The practitioner of bad faith elects to say "the devil did it to me" rather than to take responsibility for the hard and difficult choices that would create a different outcome.

Over-commitment. Over-commitment is another way in which we threaten our health and wellbeing. The failure to limit our commitments to a number that can be handled effectively places additional responsibilities onto what might be an already burdened schedule. With each additional commitment we lose time and energy that was previously devoted to others. Under these conditions, the quality with which we perform our duties begins to slip, as does our enthusiasm. You no doubt have had friends promoted to positions for which they were not prepared and who became, over a period of months, soured by the excessive demands of their new job. "He's got too much on his mind," "She takes things too seriously," "He's just not the same old guy," and so on go the descriptions of the individual overcome with commitments he or she cannot possibly meet. It's like the circus performer who tries to see how many plates he can keep spinning. His performance requires enormous energy as he continues to run back and forth giving the wobbly plates an additional spin.

Hurry sickness. A related factor is our tendency to fall prey to "hurry sickness."[13] Kenneth Pelletier, in his book, *Mind as Healer, Mind as Slayer,* defines hurry sickness as a preoccupation with what we hope or plan to do next while engaged in an activity that should absorb all of our attention.[14] In the terms of the previous chapter, it is a failure to proceed deliberately. Hurry sickness seems to have reached epidemic proportions in today's world. Automobile accidents, heart attacks, shortened tempers, sleeplessness, and indigestion are some of the symptoms of this disease. When afflicted with hurry sickness, we tend to bring deadlines to activities that should be savored. We rush through meals, lack patience with our children, and apply the time saving strategies of the work-a-day world to every hour of our day. When the condition becomes chronic, we even find ourselves hurrying through the activities devoted to self-enrichment, as if there is something else for which time should be saved.

Living in the past. Finally, just as wide spread as hurry sickness is the inclination to hold on to the past and to expect friends and familiar situations to remain unchanged. This is the mistake of Holdfast, the clown of classical mythology, who saw change as a threat to security.[15] It is not uncommon, for example, to hear individuals comment on the unfulfilled promise of adulthood, and on how they long for years gone by. Perhaps the tedium of their everyday life has caught them unprepared. They are frightened by its starkness and lack of intimacy and so they retreat in their minds to the past, to the way things used to be. This stratagem fails, however, and invariably so since each of us has (however momentarily dormant) the irrepressible desire to be a full participant in the events of our own lives. To play the role of Holdfast is to live increasingly apart from our selves, and from the present, a sure way to retard or interfere with personal growth. Holdfast experiences both the disappointment that comes from his failure to secure the past and the terror that comes from no longer being a full participant in the living of his own life. It is a formula for depression, a depression from which it is often hard to recover since Holdfast is in the habit of avoiding the present, the only place where health-renewing activity can occur.

SUMMARY

These sixteen factors were selected not only because they are common anxiety-inducing factors but because, in some cases, they are difficult to acknowledge. It's very easy, for example, to deny the presence of bad faith, over-commitment, and many of the others because they imply that we bring stress and anxiety onto ourselves by the way we think and by what we choose to do. They suggest that it is our decision to think and act as we do that makes our experience more or less anxiety-filled.

The exercises that follow the Study Guide allow you to survey many areas of your life, including the key relationships in your life. By carefully and honestly completing the exercises you will be identifying the anxiety-producing factors and/or relationships currently operating in your life.

> *NOTE: After completing the Study Guide, take your time with the exercises. They can be time-consuming to complete, and also challenging. It can be painful, for example, to review and acknowledge the degree to which certain important relationships are not working. It's here that we return to the suggestion offered in the Preface; namely, that working with a therapist or counselor can be helpful. With these exercises, and with the final chapter, you can find that you are probing deeply into your life and for some of us that can mean looking into why we might be depressed, sad, angry, perhaps addicted to some substance or activity. If that proves to be the case, then professional help can be invaluable.*

STUDY GUIDE / REVIEW

Complete each statement by filling in the blank. Return to the text for review as well as to verify the accuracy of your answers.

1. The purpose of this chapter is to help you identify your major _____.

2. By definition, these are the factors that stand between you and the _____ relaxed mode.

3. Situational factors are those factors inherent in a situation that cause it to be _____.

4. One such factor is sudden and unexpected _____.

5. Another situational factor is the blockage of _____ - directed behavior.

6. In work-related situations, where "time is money," the necessities of business bring into play a set of _____ performance pressures that also can increase stress and anxiety.

7. Another situational factor is high _____ work, work in which the consequences for error are severe.

8. Just as stressful as these jobs—at least on occasion—are those jobs that are so simple and unchallenging that _____ is inevitable.

9. Finally the lack of _____ treatment is certain work and social situations is another situational factor capable of producing tension and anxiety.

10. Social factors are those factors that influence the interpersonal buffers and supports that protect us from excessive _____.

11. One social factor contributing stress and anxiety to our lives is social _____.

12. Another is society's lack of tolerance for deviations from its socially sanctioned _____.

13. Traditionally, it has been the _____ that has protected the individual from the excessive strain of aloneness.

14. Without some version of the _____, some set of relationships in which there is permanence, trust, and unconditional support, you are forced to draw on your own resources for fortification and renewal.

15. A recent paper reviewing research on life events and illness indicates that "... social _____ has been delineated as a major factor in increased risk of disease."

16. Regardless of how it happens, as soon as your social support system weakens, so too often times your resistance to _____.

17. Personal factors are good examples of how we threaten our own _____ by behaving in irrational and irresponsible ways.

18. A common view and one that certainly can increase the stress and anxiety in one's life is to hold that you are not responsible for how you _____.

19. This is a crippling misperception because it makes you _____ on others for your sense of wellbeing.

20. It's important to remember that everything has a _____, a reason for happening.

21. It can be a waste of _____ to insist that something else should have happened.

22. To do so allows you to feel that you are a _____, and opens the door to anger and resentment.

23. It also can prevent you from taking steps to _____ a troublesome situation.

24. Another common misperception is to assume that you have no choice, "to pretend

something is necessary that in fact is _____."

25. This is referred to as bad _____.

26. Carried to its extreme, it represents an abandonment of personal _____.

27. With over-commitment comes a decline in the _____ with which you perform your duties.

28. A factor related to over-commitment is our tendency to fall prey to "_____" sickness.

29. This is defined as preoccupation with what you hope or plan to do next while engaged in an activity that should absorb all your _____.

30. Finally, just as dangerous and widespread as this sickness is the inclination to hold on to the _____ and to expect friends and familiar situations to remain unchanged.

31. This is dangerous because it prevents you from being a full participant in the events of your own _____.

32. It prevents you from living in the _____, the only place where health-renewing activity can occur.

33. The factors discussed in this chapter emphasize that it is often our decision to think and act as we do that makes the experience of everyday life more or less _____.

34. When you have finished the exercises that follow, you will have a good idea of what you need to work on in order to more closely approximate the _____ relaxed mode of performance.

Be sure you have completed all statements accurately before moving to the exercises.

EXERCISE G: Social Support Network

In this exercise you have the opportunity to map the degree to which you are satisfied with each of the relationships in your social or interpersonal network. You are asked to consider how important each relationship is to you and to consider, as well, your satisfaction with each. A relationship that is very important but with which you are not at all satisfied is likely a source of stress. If that relationship can be put right—whatever that might mean as it could mean any number of things, from a heart-to-heart talk to learning to see the relationship in a new way—then one less source of stress and anxiety will exist in your life and, perhaps, another degree of freedom added.

Instructions:

1. Complete the rows in the accompanying table by filling in the names of brothers, sisters, grandparents, aunts, uncles, children, friends, in-laws, fellow employees and others comprising your circle of family, friends, associates and acquaintances.

2. Across from each individual circle the number indicating how important this person is to you and the number indicating how satisfied you are with your current relationship with this person. (Note that the scales change. With the first question a rating of "1" means "not at all" and a rating of "5" means "extremely" while in the second question it is just the reverse. Keep this in mind while completing the table.)

3. Go back and multiply the ratings in order to obtain the score for each relationship. The higher the score, the more troublesome the relationship. For example, a score of 25 identifies a relationship that is "extremely" important to you but with which you are "not at all" satisfied.

4. Finally, indicate whether or not you think the relationship can be improved by circling either the "Y" or the "N" across from each score. If you believe that a relationship receiving a high score can be put right (in some way), thereby reducing the score *you would give it next time*, then you have potentially identified an issue to work on, a place to focus your energy in service to your own health and wellbeing (and perhaps in service to the health and wellbeing of others, as well).

	How important is this person to you?	How satisfied are you with your relationship?		Can the relationship be improved?
	Not at all ... Extremely	Not at all	Score	
Mother	1 2 3 4 5	1 2 3 4 5	____	Y N
Father	1 2 3 4 5	1 2 3 4 5	____	Y N
Spouse/Partner	1 2 3 4 5	1 2 3 4 5	____	Y N
Children:	1 2 3 4 5	1 2 3 4 5	____	Y N
_____	1 2 3 4 5	1 2 3 4 5	____	Y N
_____	1 2 3 4 5	1 2 3 4 5	____	Y N
_____	1 2 3 4 5	1 2 3 4 5	____	Y N
_____	1 2 3 4 5	1 2 3 4 5	____	Y N
_____	1 2 3 4 5	1 2 3 4 5	____	Y N
_____	1 2 3 4 5	1 2 3 4 5	____	Y N
_____	1 2 3 4 5	1 2 3 4 5	____	Y N
_____	1 2 3 4 5	1 2 3 4 5	____	Y N
Siblings:				
_____	1 2 3 4 5	1 2 3 4 5	____	Y N
_____	1 2 3 4 5	1 2 3 4 5	____	Y N
_____	1 2 3 4 5	1 2 3 4 5	____	Y N
_____	1 2 3 4 5	1 2 3 4 5	____	Y N
_____	1 2 3 4 5	1 2 3 4 5	____	Y N
_____	1 2 3 4 5	1 2 3 4 5	____	Y N
_____	1 2 3 4 5	1 2 3 4 5	____	Y N
_____	1 2 3 4 5	1 2 3 4 5	____	Y N
Relatives:				
_____	1 2 3 4 5	1 2 3 4 5	____	Y N
_____	1 2 3 4 5	1 2 3 4 5	____	Y N
_____	1 2 3 4 5	1 2 3 4 5	____	Y N
_____	1 2 3 4 5	1 2 3 4 5	____	Y N
_____	1 2 3 4 5	1 2 3 4 5	____	Y N
_____	1 2 3 4 5	1 2 3 4 5	____	Y N
_____	1 2 3 4 5	1 2 3 4 5	____	Y N
_____	1 2 3 4 5	1 2 3 4 5	____	Y N
Friends:				
_____	1 2 3 4 5	1 2 3 4 5	____	Y N
_____	1 2 3 4 5	1 2 3 4 5	____	Y N
_____	1 2 3 4 5	1 2 3 4 5	____	Y N
_____	1 2 3 4 5	1 2 3 4 5	____	Y N
_____	1 2 3 4 5	1 2 3 4 5	____	Y N
_____	1 2 3 4 5	1 2 3 4 5	____	Y N
_____	1 2 3 4 5	1 2 3 4 5	____	Y N
_____	1 2 3 4 5	1 2 3 4 5	____	Y N
_____	1 2 3 4 5	1 2 3 4 5	____	Y N

Colleagues/
co-workers

Name	Rating 1	Rating 2	Score	Y/N
_____	1 2 3 4 5	1 2 3 4 5	____	Y N
_____	1 2 3 4 5	1 2 3 4 5	____	Y N
_____	1 2 3 4 5	1 2 3 4 5	____	Y N
_____	1 2 3 4 5	1 2 3 4 5	____	Y N
_____	1 2 3 4 5	1 2 3 4 5	____	Y N
_____	1 2 3 4 5	1 2 3 4 5	____	Y N
_____	1 2 3 4 5	1 2 3 4 5	____	Y N
_____	1 2 3 4 5	1 2 3 4 5	____	Y N
_____	1 2 3 4 5	1 2 3 4 5	____	Y N

Others:

Name	Rating 1	Rating 2	Score	Y/N
_____	1 2 3 4 5	1 2 3 4 5	____	Y N
_____	1 2 3 4 5	1 2 3 4 5	____	Y N
_____	1 2 3 4 5	1 2 3 4 5	____	Y N
_____	1 2 3 4 5	1 2 3 4 5	____	Y N
_____	1 2 3 4 5	1 2 3 4 5	____	Y N
_____	1 2 3 4 5	1 2 3 4 5	____	Y N
_____	1 2 3 4 5	1 2 3 4 5	____	Y N
_____	1 2 3 4 5	1 2 3 4 5	____	Y N

Review your ratings and list below those individuals with whom you have relationships in need of your attention, relationships that you believe can be improved (scores of 25, for example).

_____

_____

If there are no relationships in need of your immediate attention, then list below the names of individuals with whom you have relationships that you would like to improve.

_____

_____

_____

EXERCISE H: "Lovers & Teachers"

"There are two kinds of people in the world: lovers and teachers. Lovers are those people who introduce you to that stuff in yourself that you absolutely love. And teachers are those people who introduce you to that stuff in yourself that you do not love. And there are no other kinds of people."

—Ken Keyes

This exercise gives you the opportunity to identify the desirable skill, trait, attitude, or behavior that you are being invited to acquire by your "teachers" (i.e., those individuals with whom you have an anxiety-provoking or stress-filled relationship). It may be courage or acceptance; it may be learning to "live and let live" or simply acquiring the assertiveness to say "no; or it may be forgiveness. Whatever it is, the presumption here is that the individuals with whom you have a difficult relationship are "teachers" (i.e., can be seen as "teachers") and that they are giving you the opportunity to learn something important and invaluable, something that will aid you in your development as a person.

Instructions:

List below the five or six individuals with the highest scores from the previous exercise. Across from each, write the skill, attitude or behavior that this person is giving you the opportunity to acquire and which, if acquired, would allow you to be more relaxed, more yourself around them.

Score	Name (initials)	Desirable skill, attitude or behavior you are being "invited" to learn or practice:
_____	_____	_____
_____	_____	_____
_____	_____	_____
_____	_____	_____
_____	_____	_____
_____	_____	_____
_____	_____	_____
_____	_____	_____

EXERCISE I: Communication Style

In the course of her work with families, American Family Therapist Virginia Satir identified what she came to believe were the five communication styles adopted by human beings. Only one of the five, she argued, was healthy. The five styles are:

1. PLEASING: Trying to please, to placate, to mediate, to patch things up so the other person doesn't get mad; it's an "I don't count, your the one who matters" attitude. "Evokes guilt so you will spare me." Leads, in the extreme, to tiredness, depression, suicide.

2. BLAMING: "Always" or "never" are frequently used words; so the other person will regard you as strong; "If it weren't for you, my life would be OK" attitude. "Evokes fear, so you will obey me." Lonely position, in the extreme, homicide.

3. COMPUTER: Preachy, knows all the answers; "should" and "ought to" frequently used words; deals with threats as though they were harmless; hides behind big words and intellectual concepts; heavy advice giving. "Evokes envy so you will ally with me." Feelings are dry and barren, leads in the extreme to an emotional death.

4. IRRELEVANT: Nothing fits; in motion; random talk; the words make no sense; behaves as if threat is not there; distracts oneself and others from reality of situation. The individual is off somewhere else. "Evokes longing for fun, so you will tolerate me." Pain so great the individual checks out, goes crazy, psychotic.

5. LEVELING: Position of high self-esteem and personal awareness. Leveling is a response, the other four are reactions. "I" statements characterize this style. The freedom to say "I see..."; "I hear..."; "I feel..."; etc. Not what I should (see, hear, feel) but what I do, in fact, see, hear, feel.

<u>Leveling invites leveling.</u>

> *"... just about everyone I have found who has serious problems coping with life—school problems, alcoholism, adultery, whatever—was communicating in the first four crippling ways . . . these four styles arise from low feelings of self-worth that we learned as children."*

—Virginia Satir
The New Peoplemaking

Instructions: On the lines provided in the left hand column, write the names/initials of the key individuals in your life. In Column I write the name of the communication style that you seem to use predominately with each of the individuals listed. In Column II, write the name of the communication style that you seem to invite from each of them (i.e., that they use with you).

Name	Column I	Column II
Mother	_____	_____
Father	_____	_____
Spouse/Sig. Other	_____	_____

Siblings:

_____	_____	_____
_____	_____	_____
_____	_____	_____
_____	_____	_____
_____	_____	_____

Children:

_____	_____	_____
_____	_____	_____
_____	_____	_____
_____	_____	_____
_____	_____	_____

Relatives:

_____	_____	_____
_____	_____	_____
_____	_____	_____
_____	_____	_____

Friends:

_____	_____	_____
_____	_____	_____
_____	_____	_____
_____	_____	_____
_____	_____	_____
_____	_____	_____

Boss; Supervisors:

_____ _____ _____
_____ _____ _____
_____ _____ _____

Colleagues:

_____ _____ _____
_____ _____ _____
_____ _____ _____
_____ _____ _____
_____ _____ _____

Co-workers:

_____ _____ _____
_____ _____ _____
_____ _____ _____
_____ _____ _____
_____ _____ _____
_____ _____ _____
_____ _____ _____

Neighbors:

_____ _____ _____
_____ _____ _____
_____ _____ _____
_____ _____ _____
_____ _____ _____

Others:

_____ _____ _____
_____ _____ _____
_____ _____ _____
_____ _____ _____
_____ _____ _____
_____ _____ _____
_____ _____ _____

EXERCISE J: Personality Characteristics

This exercise is completed in the same way as the Social Support Network Exercise, and will give you the opportunity to review your satisfaction with an array of personality characteristics.

	How important is this characteristic to you?					How satisfied are you with your level of it?					Can your level be improved?
	Not at all				Extremely	Not at all					Score
Assertiveness	1	2	3	4	5	1	2	3	4	5	____ Y N
Boldness	1	2	3	4	5	1	2	3	4	5	____ Y N
Cleanliness	1	2	3	4	5	1	2	3	4	5	____ Y N
Courage	1	2	3	4	5	1	2	3	4	5	____ Y N
Courtesy	1	2	3	4	5	1	2	3	4	5	____ Y N
Enthusiasm	1	2	3	4	5	1	2	3	4	5	____ Y N
Fairness	1	2	3	4	5	1	2	3	4	5	____ Y N
Friendliness	1	2	3	4	5	1	2	3	4	5	____ Y N
Frugality	1	2	3	4	5	1	2	3	4	5	____ Y N
Gaiety	1	2	3	4	5	1	2	3	4	5	____ Y N
Humility	1	2	3	4	5	1	2	3	4	5	____ Y N
Humor	1	2	3	4	5	1	2	3	4	5	____ Y N
Industry	1	2	3	4	5	1	2	3	4	5	____ Y N
Moderation	1	2	3	4	5	1	2	3	4	5	____ Y N
Orderliness	1	2	3	4	5	1	2	3	4	5	____ Y N
Patience	1	2	3	4	5	1	2	3	4	5	____ Y N
Resoluteness	1	2	3	4	5	1	2	3	4	5	____ Y N
Self-respect	1	2	3	4	5	1	2	3	4	5	____ Y N
Shrewdness	1	2	3	4	5	1	2	3	4	5	____ Y N
Sincerity	1	2	3	4	5	1	2	3	4	5	____ Y N
Temperance	1	2	3	4	5	1	2	3	4	5	____ Y N

Review your ratings and list below the one personality characteristic that you believe requires your attention (score of 25, for example).

_____

If none exists, then list below one characteristic you are confident of improving with a manageable degree of effort.

_____

EXERCISE K: Lifestyle Considerations

This exercise gives you an opportunity to reflect on your lifestyle, to consider whether or not certain desirable activities have been squeezed out and now must be returned in order to add fullness to your everyday life. On the blank lines at the bottom of the table, list any additional items that are important to you and answer the questions for them, as well.

	How important is this characteristic to you? Not at all — Extremely	How satisfied are you with your level of it? Not at all	Score	Can your level be improved?
Reading	1 2 3 4 5	1 2 3 4 5	____	Y N
Writing	1 2 3 4 5	1 2 3 4 5	____	Y N
Dancing	1 2 3 4 5	1 2 3 4 5	____	Y N
Singing	1 2 3 4 5	1 2 3 4 5	____	Y N
Painting	1 2 3 4 5	1 2 3 4 5	____	Y N
Traveling	1 2 3 4 5	1 2 3 4 5	____	Y N
Exercising	1 2 3 4 5	1 2 3 4 5	____	Y N
Income	1 2 3 4 5	1 2 3 4 5	____	Y N
Education	1 2 3 4 5	1 2 3 4 5	____	Y N
Watching TV	1 2 3 4 5	1 2 3 4 5	____	Y N
Gardening	1 2 3 4 5	1 2 3 4 5	____	Y N
Hygiene	1 2 3 4 5	1 2 3 4 5	____	Y N
Conversation	1 2 3 4 5	1 2 3 4 5	____	Y N
Nutrition	1 2 3 4 5	1 2 3 4 5	____	Y N
Corresponding	1 2 3 4 5	1 2 3 4 5	____	Y N
Social media	1 2 3 4 5	1 2 3 4 5	____	Y N
Politics	1 2 3 4 5	1 2 3 4 5	____	Y N
Recreation	1 2 3 4 5	1 2 3 4 5	____	Y N
Sports	1 2 3 4 5	1 2 3 4 5	____	Y N
Sex	1 2 3 4 5	1 2 3 4 5	____	Y N
Self-reliance	1 2 3 4 5	1 2 3 4 5	____	Y N
Religion	1 2 3 4 5	1 2 3 4 5	____	Y N
Nature	1 2 3 4 5	1 2 3 4 5	____	Y N
Shopping	1 2 3 4 5	1 2 3 4 5	____	Y N
Partying	1 2 3 4 5	1 2 3 4 5	____	Y N
Your weight	1 2 3 4 5	1 2 3 4 5	____	Y N
Cooking	1 2 3 4 5	1 2 3 4 5	____	Y N
Spending time with friends	1 2 3 4 5	1 2 3 4 5	____	Y N
Location of your home	1 2 3 4 5	1 2 3 4 5	____	Y N
Budgeting of your own time	1 2 3 4 5	1 2 3 4 5	____	Y N
Making your own decisions	1 2 3 4 5	1 2 3 4 5	____	Y N

Spending time with family	1	2	3	4	5	1	2	3	4	5	____	Y	N
Laughing	1	2	3	4	5	1	2	3	4	5	____	Y	N
Making others laugh	1	2	3	4	5	1	2	3	4	5	____	Y	N
Going to the movies	1	2	3	4	5	1	2	3	4	5	____	Y	N
Taking pictures	1	2	3	4	5	1	2	3	4	5	____	Y	N
Discussing feelings	1	2	3	4	5	1	2	3	4	5	____	Y	N
Meeting new people	1	2	3	4	5	1	2	3	4	5	____	Y	N
Maintaining old ties	1	2	3	4	5	1	2	3	4	5	____	Y	N
Teaching	1	2	3	4	5	1	2	3	4	5	____	Y	N
Hiking	1	2	3	4	5	1	2	3	4	5	____	Y	N
Meaningful work	1	2	3	4	5	1	2	3	4	5	____	Y	N
_____	1	2	3	4	5	1	2	3	4	5	____	Y	N
_____	1	2	3	4	5	1	2	3	4	5	____	Y	N
_____	1	2	3	4	5	1	2	3	4	5	____	Y	N
_____	1	2	3	4	5	1	2	3	4	5	____	Y	N
_____	1	2	3	4	5	1	2	3	4	5	____	Y	N
_____	1	2	3	4	5	1	2	3	4	5	____	Y	N
_____	1	2	3	4	5	1	2	3	4	5	____	Y	N

Review your ratings and list below any changes in your lifestyle that you believe require your attention (score of 25, for example).

_____

_____

If none exist, then list below any items that if attended to would improve your lifestyle, items you feel you could address with a manageable effort.

_____

_____

_____

PROGRESS CHECK

Answer the questions below as accurately as you can. When you have finished, check your answers with those supplied in the answer key.

1. The purpose of this chapter is to help you identify your sources of stress and _____.

2. The factors discussed in the text portion of this chapter were divided into situational, social and personal factors. Situational factors are those factors inherent in a situation that cause it to be _____.

3. Social factors influence the interpersonal buffers and support networks that protect us from excessive _____.

4. Personal factors are viewpoints or _____ that cause us to make neutral situations stressful.

5. Sudden and unexpected change, the blockage of goal-directed behavior, time performance pressure, the risk or tedium of certain work, and the lack of fair treatment are all _____ factors.

6. Increased mobility, deviation from socially sanctioned roles, and isolation are all _____ factors.

7. Blaming others, bad faith, over-commitment, and hurry sickness are _____ factors.

8. The exercises accompanying this chapter are designed to help you construct your _____ of major challenges (i.e., anxiety factors and/or relationships).

9. A score of 25 indicates a relationship that is extremely important to you but with which you are not at all _____.

12. "Lovers" are those people who introduce you to that stuff in yourself that you _____.

13. "Teachers" are those people who introduce you to that stuff in yourself that you do not _____.

14. It is our decision to think and act as we do that goes a long way toward making the situations and relationships we are in more or less _____.

15. Name the five communication styles identified by Virginia Satir.

    1. _____
    2. _____
    3. _____
    4. _____
    5. _____

16. Which of the five should we make the effort to practice? _____

*Check your answers against those listed in the Answer Key—
located in Appendix A*

Chapter V

Pain Drains, Addiction & the Heroic Strategy

In this last chapter we discuss a strategy for acquiring differential relaxation. It is well beyond the realm of any book to teach differential relaxation since differential relaxation is, for most of us, a skill (or style) acquired gradually over time. But a strategy for acquiring the differentially relaxed mode can be discussed. The strategy discussed here calls first for an honest self-appraisal, a review perhaps (as was done in the preceding exercises) of the habits and relationships that may be causing undo stress and anxiety in our lives; and second, a "putting right" of those issues, however that is to be done. To emphasize the difficulty of this strategy, its rarity and its promise, it is called the heroic strategy (not an overstatement when you consider that the heroic, in this context, means simply the overcoming of personal limitation). It is a strategy that stands in sharp contrast to the strategy of escape and avoidance employed by so many of us when confronted with the opportunity to deal with the issues undermining our wellbeing.

PAIN DRAINS[1]

Perhaps the most important question posed by this book is: *How do you deal with the issues, situations, and factors that bring tension and anxiety into your life, the factors that threaten your wellbeing?* The answer for most of us is that we run from them. We run from them by seeking what N. Arthur Coulter has called *pain drains*. Pain drains are pleasurable activities that allow us to escape and avoid the pain implicit in confronting the sources of our anxiety. Pain drains, therefore, are unhealthy pursuits because they take us away from the very factors with which we must deal if we are to remain well (let alone thrive).

Nearly any activity can function as a pain drain but common examples include eating, reading, TV watching, shopping, drinking, gambling. Each of these can and does provide pleasure but when sought for the wrong reason, when sought for escape, each becomes a potential trap. Consider, for example, eating. When hungry, eating is the proper response. Eating is not the proper response, however, when done for the wrong reason. How often have you found yourself in front of the refrigerator searching for an in-between-meal snack, not because you are hungry but because you are anxious. Your plan (however unconscious) is to leave the anxiety behind by escaping into food, into its tastes and textures. When successful, you will have found an escape from the depressing fact that you are anxious and perhaps bored. TV watching is another example. Some programs are entertaining, others educational, yet how often have you found yourself "planted" in front of the TV, a slave to the most inane programming? "If it will just hold my attention," you seem to be saying, "then tomorrow is another day and then, surely, I will have the time and energy to devote to my priorities." Until tomorrow, however, there are this evening's reruns followed by the Tonight Show.

Alcoholic binges, excessive reading of escape literature,[2] shopping sprees, extra-marital relationships, and numerous other activities are often pursued and repeated simply because they permit us to escape and avoid the issues making us anxious. But the escape is only momentary and that's the catch. A pain drain postpones anxiety, it does not eliminate it; it buys time, not satisfaction. Sooner or later, if the source of the anxiety amounts to anything at all, it will have to be confronted. The point being that a pain drain works only until its novelty wears off. Without novelty, the would-be (and probably over-used) pain drain loses its ability to capture and hold attention, thereby returning contact with the previously avoided anxiety.

Add to this a further complication. Pain drains create appetites where previously none existed. Artificial appetites, perhaps, but appetites all the same, ones that produce painful withdrawal cravings if not continually fed. Thus, pain drains threaten with the prospect of addiction. By trying to run away from our problems we succeed only in acquiring new ones.

ADDICTION

Based on the work of two psychologists, Richard L. Solomon and John D. Corbit, it is now reasonable to believe that psychological or behavioral addiction to activities that provide pleasure or relieve anxiety occurs as readily and in the same manner as does physiological addition to opiates.[3] Without going into their theory on the dynamics underlying addiction, it is possible, with the aid of a few examples to come to an understanding both of their work and of its implication for anyone who repeatedly chooses to escape from anxiety through the use of pain drains.

Consider the process underlying opiate addiction. For whatever reason (curiosity, thrill-seeking, escape), an individual decides to inject an opiate. The outcome of this act is best divided into two phases. The first phase, immediately following the injection, is characterized by "an intensely pleasurable feeling" called a "rush" which is directly "followed by a period of less intense euphoria."[4] The second phase occurs as the euphoria wears off and is characterized by a slight "let down" accompanied by a faint craving.

Since, on balance, the outcome of the first injection is pleasurable, the individual is likely to do it again. However, with repeated use, and this is the important point, the pleasure and euphoria associated with phase one diminishes while the force and duration of phase two, the "let down" and craving, intensifies. This process continues until the rush and euphoria of phase one becomes negligible when compared to the aversive withdrawal symptoms of phase two. It is at this point that the user consumes the drug solely for the purpose of avoiding the pangs of withdrawal. It is no longer a source of pleasure, nor is it a means for escaping anxiety, other than the anxiety produced by the symptoms of withdrawal. As Solomon and Corbit put it, "The well-addicted drug user is exhibiting avoidance behavior much of the time . . . He would rather not experience (phase two); he indulges so frequently that he rarely lets it occur, and if it occurs, he quickly gets rid of it with another dosage."[5] In other words, *the drug has become the means by which the addict avoids the anxiety resulting from the drug's absence.*

According to Solomon and Corbit, this is the process underlying not just physiological addiction but psychological and behavioral addiction as well. They argue that any activity that provides pleasure or relieves anxiety can lead to addiction and be sought not for pleasure but rather for the relief it offers from the anxiety that can come to be associated with its absence.

Television, for example, with its talk shows, sporting events, soap operas, and specials is a source of considerable pleasure and, as was suggested earlier, often is used as a pain drain. Having once proven itself as a pain drain, the likelihood increases that it will be used again for that purpose. However, the more you watch TV, the less entertaining it often becomes; its programs flowing together as fewer and fewer capture your interest. Yet, as you may have noticed, the more you watch TV, the more accustomed you are to having it on. Turning on the TV becomes one of the most automatic and predictable operations of your day. Sooner or later, however, the TV loses its power to destroy your preoccupations. It occasionally may prove entertaining but as a pain-killer it is no longer reliable. By then, however, the prospect of turning off the TV is unthinkable; *the silence would be too unsettling.* So, regardless of which teams are playing, or whether or not you've seen this week's episode of your favorite serial, the TV stays on. And it stays on not because it provides entertainment or offers escape, but because by keeping it on you avoid the anxiety that is now associated with it being off. The irony is that instead of avoiding one of your problems by using television as an *escape, you in fact add to your problems by becoming addicted to your means of escape.* The pain drain turns out to be a trap as you find your evenings and weekends locked-in to the hourly rhythm of network programming.

The pursuit of higher rank or status within your chosen field, whether sought for reasons of escape or for greater fortune and fame, can also be addictive.[6] The typical example is the professional whose home life begins to sour. Perhaps her spouse is bored and making greater demands on her time. The children may be "great" but only in small doses, while holidays and family outings are simply endured. In short, home and family are no longer where the heart is. And so, rather than putting family life in order she escapes into her career. At first she is absorbed by it. She enjoys the increasing esteem of her colleagues along with the pleasure that comes from doing her job well. Gradually, however, these satisfactions begin to diminish. Her high standard of performance is taken for granted both by herself and by her colleagues. Nevertheless, the prospect of losing her newly acquired status produces considerable anxiety and so she works hard to maintain it. At this point her effort to maintain her acquired status "seems better explained by her desire to avoid the pain of withdrawal symptoms than by her desire for any positive gratification."[7] Throughout this process her personal problems have probably worsened since her time at home has been spent thinking about work. Once again we see the irony.

Instead of avoiding her problems through work, she merely adds to their number as both she and her family come to understand what is meant by the term "workaholic."

Other examples could be added to these to further illustrate the pain drain-addiction process. Social media, in general, no doubt serves as a pain drain for some people and threatens them with the prospect of addiction. Some percentage of those suffering from obesity may have arrived at their problem by the pain drain-addiction route. Even so-called "love relationships," as Solomon and Corbit point out, are often maintained—after several years—not because of the pleasure they provide but because neither of the parties involved can bear the anxiety that would result from the dissolution of the relationship. By now, however, the point should be clear. Pain drains can lead to addiction and addiction adds to your problems. It doesn't matter whether it's television, opiates, or your career; in every case, addiction means one more factor added to, rather than subtracted from, your list of anxiety-inducing factors.

The disquieting implication of all of this is that many of us do what we do not because it brings greater wellbeing into our lives, but because it allows us to avoid the factors responsible for our anxiety. Through avoidance and escape we back ourselves into a highly predictable routine, one that we hope will carry us through the day with a minimum of anxiety and pain. And day after day, week after week, month after month, we live out that routine until eventually we are overwhelmed by the very anxiety we had hoped to avoid. That is always the outcome of the escape-avoidance strategy. It's like trying to get to your destination by running in the opposite direction. As a strategy of life, it is a dead end, one that leads over the long run to greater suffering. There is another strategy, however, that has the promise of extending the differentially relaxed mode to the full range of everyday experience. It is an active and assertive strategy calling for a direct approach to building and nurturing wellbeing. As indicated in the introduction to this chapter, it is called the heroic strategy.

THE HEROIC STRATEGY

Put simply, the heroic strategy means: *a committed approach to addressing the factors that limit your development as a person, that limit your wellbeing.* This is a dramatic departure from the strategy and approach assumed by so many of us. As noted above, we all too often eat because we are bored, over-commit because we lack assertiveness, and blame others for our unhappiness because we don't want the responsibility ourselves. Rather than face up to our problems, we choose to avoid them, naively preferring the practice of bad faith or the role of Holdfast to whatever may come from the struggle with personal limitation. In so doing, we adopt evasion and retreat as our strategy of life, a strategy that soon proves itself a more distorted problem than any problem it was designed to avoid.

With this we come to the fundamental irony so seldom noted in texts on relaxation, anxiety-reduction, or stress management; *namely, we cannot avoid the factors bringing stress and anxiety into our lives. We must address them in some fashion if we are truly interested in being "at ease with ourselves".* In other words, we must identify and address the relationships, the habits, the ways of thinking and doing responsible for our anxiety and lack of wellbeing. And we must continue to do so until gradually, increasingly, we are at ease with ourselves in an ever wider circle of people, situations, and settings. The differentially relaxed mode is earned. It is the result of our effort to put right the issues that currently have the power to cause us distress. It involves work on ourselves primarily, for some of us a daunting task given how entrenched in our ways we have become. The 'ruts" and "lock-ins", referred to earlier, can run deep and freeing ourselves from them no easy task. This is the sense in which the term "heroic" is appropriate. It captures the size and nature of the task in front of us. It is also appropriate because the benefits of our effort are not ours alone but flow as well to the social networks (families, workplaces, etc.) of which we are a part.

In specific terms, the heroic strategy asks us to work through our curriculum of anxiety-inducing factors (many of which were identified in Exercises C, D, E, F, and G) one item at a time. For some people, this will seem a possibility, for others, a prospect of overwhelming proportion. In either case, the task is to begin, to set out, to take one of the factors that limits freedom by imposing anxiety and to work on it, to change it: *which means, of course, to change—quite possibly—what you are doing, your thinking, your openness to and acceptance of others; it likely means—at least on some occasions—making difficult, even uncomfortable decisions.* The important thing is to take the step, no matter how small, that leads to the freeing of yourself from unnecessary—sometime self-imposed—anxiety and distress. To begin, that's the point, thereby placing your self on what some have called "the critical path."

It's impossible to say where to begin. Everyone has a different first step. The selection of what to address and how to address it is a matter best left to the honesty and ingenuity of each individual. As a general strategy, however, it makes sense to work on one item at a time and to start out gradually; working for a refinement you are confident of obtaining. This, of course, may not be possible. The time may have come "to lose that weight or else;" or there may be a key relationship so sorely in need of repair that to work on anything else is more avoidance. If that is the case then you will have to "dive in" even though the water seems over your head. Of comfort should be the fact that most of us are capable of addressing our own problems. We merely need to think through the issue and then act, proceeding humbly and with openness. The fact that we often choose not to do this should not be construed to mean we cannot do it. But if we can't, there now exists innumerable aids to assist us, from self-help books and support groups, to counselors, therapists, and the local mental health center. But whatever the course (alone or with help) and whatever the issue (weight loss, interpersonal relationship, etc.) the choice is always the same. When confronted with an anxiety-provoking, self-limiting situation we can either change our relationship to the situation, or we can change our way of looking at it. And in either case, when successful, we will be overcoming the resistances and habits within ourselves that prevent us from doing or seeing in self-beneficial ways. That is the essence of the heroic strategy: the addressing and overcoming of one's own impedances, the outcome of which is the making of a less fearful, more relaxed self.

There are three very distinct advantages to the heroic strategy. The first is that the heroic strategy has as its chief ally our ability to rationally analyze problems. Just as the "all is not well" signal exists to help us identify anxiety-inducing factors, so our ability to reason exists, at least in part, to help us solve the problems posed by those factors. If a problem appears at first unsolvable then it can be re-stated until it is in a solvable form. With each solution we not only eliminate a source of anxiety but we also gain valuable information about ourselves, information that can then be used to our advantage in the defining and solving of subsequent problems.[8]

Thus, the heroic strategy provides a rather direct approach to the ageless requirement that we know ourselves. With each problem we solve (or attempt to solve) comes self-understanding. The solving of personal problems always provides clarity on who and what we are and in what areas our strengths and weaknesses lie. This is an additional reason for adopting the heroic strategy. With its emphasis on the analysis and solution of personal problems, it offers a direct route to self-knowledge. And with self-knowledge, won in this fashion, comes self-esteem.

Ernest Becker once wrote: "man needs self-esteem more than anything."[9] It is, he said, a "universal hunger." The adoption of the heroic strategy implies a struggle—perhaps a continuing struggle—with entrenched habits, with our resistance to change even when we know that change is needed. That's why Emerson noted that the heroic consists in "always doing what you are afraid to do."[10] Yet, increasing mastery over our selves is the surest way to a lasting self-esteem. Consider, for example, the individual who successfully confronts his obesity and loses a hundred pounds, or the individual who confronts her drug addiction and "kicks it." We've all known smokers who have stopped smoking and alcoholics who have stopped drinking. Consider also the paraplegics who learn to drive, the mentally challenged who learn to read, the depressed and antisocial individual who decides to open herself to others. All represent triumphs. The fact that we don't see them as such is an indication of how long we've been confused about the nature of the heroic. It means simply, triumph over personal limitation, mastery of the self. And it has as its byproduct the production of individuals who like themselves. That's what the heroic strategy does—as hard and as frightening as it sometimes is—it gives us legitimate, life-long reasons for liking, admiring, enjoying ourselves; and so, in this way, as well, contributes to our sense of wellbeing.

Finally, the heroic strategy offers another advantage. It makes scapegoating[11] untenable. Scapegoating is a complex process involving the blaming of others for the dissatisfaction we feel with our own lives. Once we are able to believe that someone else is responsible for our discontent, it becomes very easy to dislike, even hate that person. It then is reasonable to do anything and everything we can to discredit that person, discredit them in our own mind if not in the minds of others. At that point, the scapegoating response takes the form of a cause, one to which we may devote ourselves without hesitation. Of course, scapegoating does bring pain to others, but it is a pain that we believe is justified because of the pain they bring to us. In reality, however, scapegoating stands as an elaborate pain drain. It represents the length to which we are willing to go to avoid responsibility for our own experience. It allows us to invent a cause for our own suffering, a cause that exists outside of ourselves and, once invented, to spend our time and energy doing battle in one way or another with this fabricated architect of our discontent. It is a marvelous pain drain, an ingenious mechanism for avoiding personal responsibility. Yet, the heroic strategy undercuts even this. Implicit in the heroic strategy is the notion that each of us is responsible to a considerable extent for our own experience. Success, even slight success in dealing with personal problems—especially problems previously avoided by the scapegoating response—undermines the credibility of the notion that others are responsible. It pulls the logic out from under this last defense. And the only thing that remains is a logic arguing for the continued work on oneself. This is the final advantage offered by the heroic strategy. It builds a commitment to the heroic. And it builds this commitment by stripping away the illusion that anything less than the heroic is appropriate.

(There is a proviso required here: There are of course victims in this world. There are factors over which we have little or no control and these factors can and do affect our lives dramatically. The heroic strategy and this book in general are nevertheless arguing for an approach that maximizes personal responsibility. Rather than prematurely concluding that one is a victim of larger forces (perhaps oppressive, perhaps indifferent), here the assumption is that what happens to us and/or how we choose to respond to what happens to us is more often in our own hands than we sometimes care to acknowledge.)

CONCEPT FORMATION

In the introduction to his book, *Mother Night,* Kurt Vonnegut wrote, "We are what we pretend to be, so we must be careful about what we pretend to be."[12] To elaborate, it might be said that the more we pretend, the better we become at what we pretend until the objective observer no longer can recognize the slightest sign of what is commonly called "pretense." At that point it is as though we are the very person we have pretended to be. We have behaved ourselves into it; we are at last what we have prematurely (perhaps with embarrassment) tended to be. And so, we must choose carefully, consciously, what we are willing to pretend to be.

When a man prepares for battle, he pretends to be a soldier. (To pretend anything else would be careless.) But it is not until battle, where he must fight for his life, that he becomes what he pretends to be. Having thus tasted of battle, to carry this particular analogy one step further, he now may know a tension and fear like none he has ever known. The prospect of returning to battle may paralyze him, court-martial and imprisonment, if necessary, preferred over battle. But if he is to be a soldier, he returns. And in returning, over and over again, he learns more about the management of his fear, more about the mental self-government required to survive until, at last, he drops his fear. He may still feel it, he no doubt does, but it no longer has the same power over him. It no longer can incline him toward acts that, under the circumstances, can cost him his life. In a very real sense, he has become fearless. Through battle after battle, as he saw himself survive one harrowing situation after another, a new concept of himself began to form, one consistent with his performance. At some point he had it—the fourth skirmish, the eighth. Eventually enough bases got covered, enough weakness and self-doubt overcome, permitting a new figure to stand forth, one that in time he recognized and regarded as himself.[13]

The heroic strategy prescribes a course similar to the one faced by the soldier (not as daunting, certainly; that should be acknowledged). If pursued, it serves to place the individual in one situation after another wherein he (or she) must face his fear. The pace is up to the individual and no doubt at first he must pretend to be something he does not altogether believe himself to be. (He must assume himself capable of things he may not believe he is capable of doing.) But if he persists, he stands a chance of earning and forming a new view of himself, one consistent with his performance. It may not happen. Retreat is always possible. He may, for example, attempt to put right one or two relationships and find that the effort is too great, leading him to leave things (including himself) as they are. But if he persists, meeting with some success along the way, the witnessing of his own effort will change his view of himself. He no longer sees a person who avoids and escapes the demands of what he believes to be his proper course of action. His fears and anxieties no longer seem to have the power to incline him toward acts that cost him his self-esteem. He is more and more at ease with himself because when push comes to shove he behaves in a self-respecting way. He finds that he is confident. A new self-image has been formed. And it has been formed through the successful confronting of one anxiety-inducing situation after another. Maybe it was the fourth situation, or the twelfth—at some turn the pattern was complete and with it came a new and preferred sense of self.

The important thing to remember is that this forming of a new or preferred self is the outcome of a specific process, a concept formation process. It is a process in which the witnessing of one's effort (and success) in the face of anxiety and fear in dozens of specific instances induces a new concept of the self. The heroic strategy is a concept formation process. It teaches courage and self-respect in the same way that a box of sixty-four crayons teaches the concept color. At some point, the child, with very little prompting, realizes that red, green, blue, and yellow have only one thing in common: *color*. A new concept is formed. When other crayons or other objects, for that matter, are put before the child, though their names are unknown, the child recognizes that they, too, have a property called *color*. So, too, with the heroic strategy: Once the new concept is earned, *the effect generalizes,* and the individual no longer is deterred so readily by fear, nor paralyzed by what previously was experienced as the anxiety inherent in the situation. Specific anxiety-inducing situations not addressed initially (situations that previously would have been avoided out of anxiety and fear) have now lost their power to deter his movement and are dealt with as they come along. The individual moves forward with a capacity that inclines him toward success. Having overcome so often the limitations imposed by anxiety and self-doubt, he now believes himself capable of creating a peaceful or harmonious or honorable solution whatever the situation.

The fact that the heroic strategy is a concept formation process means that not every item identified in the self-review undertaken at the end of Chapter IV must be addressed: Only the number required in order for *the effect to take hold and generalize.* That is, only the number required in order for you to feel capable of dealing with comparably difficult situations. From that point, you deal with those situations as they come along and you do so with far less anxiety and consternation. This is how we grow (one of the ways we grow); we behave our way into an increased capacity to deal with difficult situations. And we do so by successfully dealing with several situations until we have become a person who can handle that degree of difficulty. Yes, there may be other more difficult situations to address, the next level of difficulty, so to speak, but dealing with them successfully is now more likely given our increased capacity. Though the task of acquiring and maintaining the differentially relaxed mode is difficult, it is not at all impossible. As noted above, not all the items identified in the self-review must be addressed, just the number required to induce the next meaningful degree of wherewithal. That is noteworthy. It means that what may have appeared impossible—acquiring the "at ease with ourselves" mode of being—is, in fact, doable. For many people, it is only a few steps away and then, perhaps, as the readiness for greater wellbeing increases, another few steps as the range over which one can operate with ease and effectiveness expands.

SOCIAL RESPONSIBILITY

Albert Nock, in his *Memoirs of a Superfluous Man,* wrote: "the only thing that the psychically-human being can do to improve society is to present society with one improved unit."[14] One of the operating assumptions of this book has been that the heroic strategy, with its emphasis on addressing in some fashion the factors that impose anxiety, stress, and fear is a socially responsible strategy. Socially responsible in the sense Nock describes, in the sense that, if embraced, it results in (and therefore allows the individual to present society with) "an improved and improving unit." The individual who has worked to put his life together has not behaved in a socially irresponsible manner. His selfishness, if it can be called that, has not been of the sort that leads to a weakened social fabric wherein more and more the experience of the individual (i.e., the single unit) is that of a social isolate. Rather, the emphasis has been on the overcoming of those factors within oneself that serve to isolate the individual against his or her will; the factors that operate against successful interpersonal relationships and a strengthened social fabric. The more such individuals a society has, and this was Nock's point, the stronger that society is likely to be. Such individuals, to put it differently, are civilizing forces, refining themselves and, by their example, inviting, encouraging, and mildly pressuring others to do the same. While there may be more that an individual can do to improve society, this alone seems meaningful; and elegant, because here the serving of others is the natural by-product of the effort to improve oneself.

STUDY GUIDE / REVIEW

Complete each statement by filling in the blank. Return to the text for review as well as to verify the accuracy of your answers.

1. Differential relaxation is characterized by a noise-free _____.

2. It also is characterized by a deliberate or _____ approach to the issues of daily life.

3. Differential relaxation is not so much a skill as it is a _____.

4. The strategy for acquiring the differentially relaxed mode is called the _____ strategy.

5. This strategy stands in sharp contrast to the _____-_____ strategy employed by many of us when confronted with the opportunity to deal with anxiety-inducing factors.

6. Pain drains are pleasurable activities that allow us to _____ the pain implicit in confronting the sources of our anxiety.

7. Eating, reading, TV watching, drug taking, shopping, drinking, gambling, and numerous other activities are often pursued and repeated simply because they permit us to _____ from the issues making us anxious.

8. Some pain drains are capable of creating an appetite where none previously existed. These appetites can produce painful _____ cravings if not continually fed.

9. Thus, some pain drains threaten with the prospect of _____.

10. Thus, the irony of the escape-avoidance strategy is that instead of avoiding one of your problems through escape, you _____ to your problems by becoming addicted to your means of escape.

11. The purpose of this chapter is to help you identify your major _____.

12. The heroic strategy requires that you address in some fashion the factors responsible for your _____.

13. The major paradox of this book is that conflict, anxiety and tension cannot be avoided, not entirely, if you are truly interested in being at _____ with yourself.

14. To work on and overcome the factors that inhibit your freedom by imposing anxiety means that you sometimes must change _____.

15. It's impossible to say where to begin when addressing your anxiety-inducing factors. Everyone has a different first step though it does make sense to work on _____ item or issue at a time.

16. It also makes sense to start with an issue or item you are _____ you can address successfully.

17. As you succeed with the issues/relationships/etc. that you believe you must address, you will be gaining important information about _____.

18. With each issue addressed comes an increase in _____-_____.

19. Ernest Becker wrote that "man needs _____-_____ more than anything.

20. The heroic strategy has as its byproduct the production of individuals who increasingly _____ themselves.

21. The heroic strategy makes the _____ response less and less tenable.

22. Implicit in the heroic strategy is the notion that each of us is responsible (not entirely, perhaps, but to a considerable degree) for our own _____.

23. A new and improved _____-_____ is formed as the individual successfully addresses the anxiety-inducing situations in his/her life.

24. Alfred Nock wrote: "the only thing that the psychically-human being can do to improve society is to present society with one _____ unit."

Be sure you have completed all statements accurately before moving to the exercises.

EXERCISE L: Pain Drains & Addiction

Pain Drains are those activities that allow us to escape and avoid the pain implicit in confronting the sources of our anxiety. Common pain drains include eating, reading, sleeping, gambling, drinking, shopping, drug-taking.

What are the activities, if any, that you seek out when you are in need of a pain drain?

_____

_____

_____

_____

The problem with pain drains is that they can lead to addiction and addiction always adds to, it never subtracts from, the list of factors that limit freedom by imposing tension, stress, and anxiety.

List below (use abbreviations, if you wish) those substances, activities, and/or people to whom, in your best judgment, you are addicted (i.e., for whom you have developed an unhealthy and powerful need). *Twelve-step programs are in every community and they have helped thousands of people deal successfully with their addictions.*

_____

_____

_____

_____

EXERCISE M: Forgiveness

One of the keys to the differentially relaxed mode, the "at ease with yourself" mode, is the capacity—little developed in most of us—to *let the past be past* Some argue that the seriousness of so many adults is due to just that, to the inability to be done with "it", *whatever it is,* in mind, heart, stomach and muscle, until the past no longer has the power to weigh down the soul with anger, resentment, and shame. Forgiveness is the term that is used.

Forgiveness can be controversial. In some instances, individuals have had the unspeakable done to them; done by adults, by neighbors, or by parents, men and women who should have known better and still they proceeded. *Forgive them? Why?*

But we arc not talking here about *forgetting.* We are talking about *forgiving,* and not for others so much as for ourselves. The advantages of forgiving belong to those willing to do it; and these advantages are doubled when we can turn this generosity inward and forgive ourselves.

It is not uncommon to hear individuals say that they can forgive everyone else but not themselves. After all, look at the suffering we have cause others and often they were the individuals we said we loved. We were negligent or we were deliberate but in either case we caused others to suffer. *Forgive ourselves? Not on your life!*

But once again, we are not talking about forgetting and thereby running the risk of repeating our mistakes. We are talking about forgiving… forgiving so that the past can be past, so that we can obtain a little more "lightness of being." To truly forgive is to take the weight off. Forgiveness lightens the load, allowing us to relax more deeply because we are carrying less.

Instructions:

1) OBJECTIFY[15]

Complete the table that follows. Enter the names (initials) of those who caused you harm. Detail (in your shorthand) what they did to you. Get it all down. And then, if you can, indicate what you learned from the experience. I know this sounds fanciful but think about it. In some cases, you learned keenness, alertness of mind, a willingness, against all odds, to make it on your own; maybe you learned to discharge anger constructively, to minimize time spent in self-pity; at the very least, you now are learning forgiveness. The fact that you had to learn these things under unfortunate circumstances is beside the point. All that matters now is that you recognize that you have turned injury to your advantage, that you did not let it happen to you without learning something of benefit from it.

Then, list your own offenses. Get them out and put them down (again in your shorthand). Experience your feelings as you put them to paper. <u>*Notice what you notice*</u>*. For all of this the proper mood is helpful, while also keeping your body as relaxed as possible. Note the muscles as they tighten and the feelings of anxiety as they arise. And then, when you have listed your own offenses, indicate what you have* *learned from them, e.g., to think before I speak, to never again make such a blunder, to fully respect myself. If nothing else, you can write forgiveness.*

2) RELEASE & FORGIVE

For many, a useful next step is to share your list: To find a counselor or therapist, for example, someone who has your very best interest in mind, and to share your list. And then to work with that person, if that person is a therapist or counselor, in whatever way the two of you believe is best suited to the forgiveness process.

If the right person is not available, or if you wish to proceed on your own then go down your list forgiving each and every person in turn including yourself. Say quietly: "I forgive you (name of the person) for what you did. I accept that it happened (whatever it was). It may have been terribly wrong but I no longer wish to hold on to the feelings associated with it. I forgive you and I forgive myself. I'm tired of the anger and the resentment. I'm done with it. I wish you the best and I am grateful for what I was able to learn from the experience. I am a stronger person now. Craft your own statement; make it detailed and earnest.

And then, release the feelings associated with the event(s) in question. Say: "And now I totally release the anger, fear, worry, shame and guilt associated with these past events. I release these feelings from my muscles, my stomach, my mind and my heart. I give them up.

If need be, give your negative and limiting feelings to something larger than yourself, to the sun perhaps, or the moon, or the Great Spirit; to something for whom such feelings are properly negligible.

Do this process daily, repeating it for three to four weeks perhaps, and each time you do it, do it with solemnity, earnestness, and a tone of insistence. Dramatize it. Ritualize it. When you use the term "release", actually release the tension in your muscles (as you have learned to do) and feel it leave. Allow yourself, for a moment, to go limp as though a great weight has been removed. Then visualize the tightness and heaviness of your stomach, heart, and mind releasing and leaving, as well. It is your capacity to perform with conviction here that is crucial . . . so that you can release what you now are convinced are feelings that serve no end to which you are committed.

AN ADDITIONAL STEP

The above process is not an elaborate mind game. It is one way of addressing your own wellbeing, and the price you (and your body) are paying as a result of the harm you have experienced and perhaps delivered. It is about moving on a wiser and more conscious person.

However, there are additional steps that can aid the forgiveness process, from the dramatic release of long pent-up feelings in a therapeutic setting, to a face-to-face exchange with the parties in question. In the latter case, perhaps, dramatizing to yourself in no uncertain terms that you are capable of standing your ground, releasing your anger or sadness constructively, and/or apologizing sincerely with the ability to hear the pain of others—as the case may require. This additional step, however, can be aided by a skilled therapist or counselor, someone or some group who can provide you with the support and guidance you may need.

Name/initials of individual (or your own name)	The event that cause you pain and/or harm (or that you did to someone else).	Have you found peace with it? What have you been able to learn from it.

EXERCISE N: Choice and Responsibility

The focus of this exercise is on *choice*. Of all the concepts that we have considered, choice is the most crucial. To the extent that you can apply this concept to yourself, apply it in the thorough fashion discussed below, to that extent you will accelerate your movement into the "at ease with yourself" mode. For choice is both the concept and the mechanism by which you increasingly make your experience your responsibility.

Choice, as the concept is used here, means that a great deal of what is currently in your life is a result of the choices you have made over the days, weeks, months, and years of your life. It is certainly true that you did not choose where you were born or to whom. Nor did you choose your early childhood or adolescent experiences. And it is also true that there are larger societal forces—social, economic, and political—that have their say, influencing the choices or options available to you at any given time. All of that is true. Still, since you have become an adult, the choices that you have made have gone a long way toward creating the situation in which you find yourself.

This can be an uncomfortable line of thought, but it is drawn in this way in order to heighten awareness and expand our sense of responsibility. Here's a possible scenario: Perhaps you find yourself in a job that no longer holds your interest. The pay may be adequate, the working environment fine, but at some level you know it is no longer for you. Imagine further that you are in a meeting with your colleagues and/or workmates while your boss rants and raves about the problems he or she faces and suddenly you notice that you have stopped yourself from saying what used to be right on the tip of your tongue: "*How can we make this better? What can we do to eliminate this problem so that we can make this workplace run smoothly and more effectively for all of us?*" At that moment, you were, in effect, *choosing* not to be there, you were choosing to leave. And thereafter, day after day, to the extent that you continued to hold back, you were choosing to exit just as surely as a man or woman "fed up" and walking out the door. Until, at last, you were so removed, so obviously removed that your boss asks you to resign *when, in fact, you had done that weeks ago!*

A similar scenario could be constructed to account for our history of failed relationships, our history of failed undertakings, our history of stress-related symptoms and disorders. Through hundreds of choices, choices with respect to what we ate, whether or not we exercised, how we treated ourselves, whether or not we remained focused, faithful, willing to face the painful issues, through hundreds of such choices we brought forward (or helped to bring forward) the extenuating circumstances that surround us.

With the concept of choice, we take responsibility for our situation, for changing it, if we believe we should, or for accepting it without recrimination or resentment, if that is the proper course. We take responsibility for defusing it of its power to keep us from being at ease with ourselves. To put it another way, we empower ourselves with the willingness to make the many choices over time that may be required to make the change we are after. We awaken—perhaps through our history of disappointment and suffering—to our role as self-responsible agents.

This is the promise and possibility embedded in the concept of choice. And it has been one of the key concepts underlying this book; namely, that *"whether we made our own beds or not, we can, in many instances, get out of them. We have the capacity to do so if we so choose."* To presume otherwise is, in all likelihood, "bad faith." From the moment that choice is fully and *consciously* embraced, then all that we have discussed becomes increasingly possible. We can *choose* for it to be so (choosing over and over again throughout each day, in the small and large ways that matter) ...and having so chosen, find ourselves with fewer excuses, less scapegoating, and less bad faith. The embracing of choice emphasizes commitment and creativity. It makes it less likely that we will keep ourselves from the experiences of life we desire most.

Instructions:

"Perfection," wrote Ken Carey, "is not the absence of mistakes, but rather the absence of conscious mistakes."[16] This exercise is an attempt to *operationalize* this important thought.

The procedure is simple. It involves counting the number of conscious mistakes made each day and plotting them on a graph.

Carry a small note pad with you or a small counter. Every time you engage in a conscious mistake, make a checkmark or click the counter. Then, at the end of the day, plot the total on your graph and write a note or two about why you elected to engage in a conscious mistake.

Now, what are conscious mistakes? Every time you eat something you have decided you should not eat, that is a conscious mistake. Also, every time you say or do something you have decided you should not say or do; or the reverse, every time you fail to say or do what you have decided you should say or do. A conscious mistake is knowing that what you are about to do is wrong, a mistake, and doing it anyway. Mistakes are fine. Mistakes are how we learn. But to know that what you are about to do is wrong, no question about it, and to do it anyway… that is a conscious mistake.

To become conscious of conscious mistakes is the outcome produced by this exercise. That and one other... If you stay with this exercise, continuing to count and plot your conscious mistakes, continuing as well to understand why you chose to do them, then you will begin to see your conscious mistakes decrease in frequency. There may be days when you set record highs but overall the rate will go down. And it will go down because lasting pleasure/happiness/self-esteem—as many philosophers agree—comes from conduct in accord with principle, conduct in accord with what you know is right for you, conduct in accord with your values. Such conduct is life-affirming, self-honoring. Conscious mistakes, on the other hand, are self-destructive.

This exercise will assist you greatly in your effort to achieve the aims of this book (providing you agree with them). Your task is to begin counting and charting. By so doing you will bring yourself into the role of pilot, navigating your way to smaller and more acceptable discrepancies while enjoying more often the ride that results.

*"Which ship goes most often onto the rocks,
the drifting ship or the ship with a pilot?"*

EXERCISE O: Sharing Your Gifts/Talents/Knowledge

"This, after all is said and done, is the only real problem of life, the only worthwhile preoccupation of man (or woman): What is (your) true talent, (your) secret gift, (your) authentic vocation? In what way (are you) truly unique, and how can (you) express this uniqueness, give it form, dedicate it to something beyond (yourself)? How can (you) take (your) private inner being, the great mystery that (you) feel at the heart of (yourself), (your) emotions, (your) yearnings, and use them to live more distinctively, to enrich both (yourself) and (humankind) with the peculiar quality of (your) talent"

—Ernest Becker
The Denial of Death

This is the final exercise and consideration of this book. You cannot feel at ease with yourself, relaxed in body and soul, unless you are fulfilling your purpose, unless you are acquiring a sense of meaning from your life. That means that you must somehow find a way to share your unique knowledge, talents and/or gifts in a way that enriches the lives of others, at least one other. This is essential. Without this in your life, you will feel restless. You will lack a level of inner peace necessary for the realization of the differentially relaxed mode.

So, what are your gifts and/or talents? What are you particularly good at, the thing (or things) that come naturally to you, or that you have worked hard to develop and now enjoy and take pride in? It does not have to be some grand talent or gift, merely what is unique to you and if shared, could enrich your life and the life of at least one other person? What are your gifts, talents, insights, and/or unique knowledge?

_____
_____
_____
_____

Are you currently sharing your gifts/talents (your uniqueness) in your personal and/or professional life? In what way? If not, how could you begin?

_____
_____
_____
_____
_____
_____
_____

PROGRESS CHECK

Answer the questions below as accurately as you can. When you have finished, check your answers with those supplied in the answer key - Appendix A.

1. Differential relaxation is characterized by a noise-free _____.

2. The strategy for becoming differentially relaxed requires an honest appraisal of personal _____.

3. The strategy for acquiring the differentially relaxed mode is called the _____ strategy.

4. Pain drains are pleasurable activities that allow us to _____ the pain implicit in confronting the sources of our anxiety.

5. The problem with pain drains is that they can lead to artificial appetites which, if not fed, can lead to painful withdrawal cravings. Thus, pain drains can lead to _____.

6. The irony of the escape-avoidance strategy is that instead of avoiding one of your problems through escape, you _____ to your problems by becoming addicted to your means of escape.

7. Conflict, anxiety and tension cannot be avoided if you are truly interested in becoming at _____ with yourself.

8. The heroic strategy has as its by-product the production of individuals who _____ themselves.

9. Blaming others for the dissatisfaction we feel with our own situation is called _____.

10. One of the keys to the lightness and freedom of the differentially relaxed mode is learning to let the past be _____.

11. This is accomplished through _____.

12. Choice is the mechanism by which you take _____ for your experience.

13. Perfection," to quote Ken Carey, "is not the absence of mistakes, but rather the absence of _____ mistakes.

14. For your sense of personal meaning, it is important that you share your unique knowledge/talents/gifts with at least _____ other person for their benefit.

Check your answers against those listed in the Answer Key— located in Appendix A.)

REFERENCES

CHAPTER I

1. Jacobson, Edmund, *You Must Relax.* New York: McGraw Hill Book Co., Inc., 1962. Much that is known about the science and practice of relaxation is due to the work of Edmund Jacobson.

2. The following is an elaboration of an analogy first suggested by John R. Platt. See Platt, John R., *Perception and Change: Projections for Survival.* Ann Arbor: The University of Michigan Press, 1970, page 143. Also, for a further discussion of lock-ins or traps, see Platt, John R., "Social Traps." American Psychologist, August, 1973.

3. Selye, Hans, *Stress Without Distress.* New York: Signet Books, 1974. The work of Selye has been one of the keys to understanding the relationship of stress to disease.

4. Holmes, Thomas H. and Masuda, Minoru, "Life change and illness susceptibility." In *Separation and Depression,* AAAS Publication No. 94, 1973, 161-186.

5. Selye, Hans, *Stress Without Distress.* New York: Signet Books, 1974

6. *ibid.*

7. Simeons, A.T.W., *Man's Presumptuous Brain.* New York: E.P. Dutton and Co., Inc., 1962.

CHAPTER II

1. See, for example, Jacobson, Edmund, *Modem Treatment of Tense Patients.* Springfield, Ill.: Charles C. Thomas, 1970. And Schultz, J.H. and Luthe, W., *Autogenic Therapy.* New York: Grune and Stratton, 1969, (Vols., I - III).

2. Jacobson, Edmund, *You Must Relax.* New York: McGraw Hill Book Co., Inc., 1962, P. 63.

3. *ibid*

4. Jourard, Sidney M., "Psychology of transcendent behavior." In *Explorations on Human Potentialities,* edited by Herbert A. Otto, Springfield, Ill.: Charles C. Thomas Inc., 1971, p. 365.

5. *ibid*

6. Campbell, Joseph, *Myths to live By,* New York: Bantam Books, 1973, p. 121.

CHAPTER III

1. Edmund Jacobson, in his previously referenced *You Must Relax*, defines differential relaxation as "the minimum of tensions in the muscles requisite for an act, along with relaxation of other muscles." p. 129. Differential relaxation is defined in slightly different terms in this chapter but in terms, I believe, consistent with Jacobson's definition.

2. Jourard, Sidney M. *The Transparent Self.* Princeton, New Jersey: D. Van Nostrand Co., Inc., 1964, p. 143.

3. *ibid*, p. 146.

4. "Noise machine" is Robert de Ropp's phrase. He introduces it in his book, *The Master Game*. New York: Delacorte Press, 1968, p.74. His chapter entitled, "The silent world," is excellent and proved most useful in the writing of this section and the section on "Deliberate Living."

5. *ibid*

6. *ibid*

7. de Roppe recommends three general techniques for reducing noise. "Undertake some physical task," he writes, "the more vigorous the better. Chop firewood, dig the garden, dance the *gopak*, climb the Sierras." When this is not possible, he recommends activities involving "repetition," as in a prayer or mantra where a single syllable or brief phrase is repeated over and over, or "visualization," as in the focusing of attention on a fixed point within a diagram or picture. See pages 88-91.

8. *ibid*, p.76.

9. Budzynski, Thomas H., Biofeedback procedures in the clinic. In Seminars in Psychiatry, November, 1973, p. 540.

10. *ibid*

11. See footnote 1 for this chapter.

12. Rajneesh, Bhhagwan Shree, *Only One Sky*. New York: E.P. Dutton and Co., 1976. (I'm aware that Rajneesh was revealed to be a notorious fellow. Even so, I found his distinction between "action" and "activity" quite helpful in the writing of this section.)

13. *ibid*, p. 73.

14. *ibid*

15. *ibid*, p. 81.

16. de Ropp, p. 85.

17 *ibid*, p. 86.

18 Eliot, T. S., Four *Quartets*. New York: Harcourt, Brace and Co., 1939, p. 10. 20-de Ropp, p. 85-86.

19 de Ropp, p. 85-86. Obviously, this example could be reversed. The wife or partner could be in the garden and upon entering the house gets into a quarrel that leads to forgetfulness and the loss of intention.

20 *ibid*, p. 86.

21 *ibid*

22 *ibid*

23 Selver, Charlotte, "Awaking the Body." In *Sources,* edited by Theodore Roszak, New York: Harper and Row Publishers, 1972, p. 175.

24 *ibid*

25 Wells, Katharine F., *Posture Exercise Handbook: A Progressive Sequence Approach.* New York: The Ronald Press Company, 1963, p. 3.

26 *ibid*

27 For instance, see Prudden, Bonnie, *How to Keep Your Family Fit and Healthy.* New York: Reader's Digest Press, 1975. And Beck, Toni and Swank, Patsy, *Focus Your Figure: A Personal Program for Natural Exercise.* Boston: Houghton Mifflin Company, 1972. Also, see the already referenced book by Wells.

28 Items 1 through 8 are taken from Wells, p. 4.

29 Hunrichsen, Gerda, *The Body Shop.* New York: Taplinger Publishing Co., 1974, p. 59.

30 *ibid*, p. 61.

31 ibid

32 John, Bubba Free, Conscious Exercise. In "East West: Common Sense for Modern Times," 8, May, 1978, p. 67.

33 Hunrichsen, p. 61.

34 *ibid*, p. 63.

35 *ibid*

36 *ibid*, p. 74.

37 *ibid*, p. 73.

38 *ibid,* p. 75.

39 *ibid,* p. 78.

40 *ibid,* p. 78-79.

CHAPTER IV

1   This breakdown into situational, social and personal factors comes from an article entitled, "Life Events, Stress, and Illness" by Judith G. Rabkin and Eµner L. Struening (see *Science,* 194, Dec. 3, 1976, p. 1013-1020). However, the anxiety factors discussed in this chapter and under the heading of these three categories are not taken from the Rabkin and Struening article.

2   DuBos, Rene, *Man Adapting.* New York: Yale University Press, 1972, p. 62.

3   *ibid,* p. 30.

4   Kafka, Franz, *The Trial.* New York: Random House, 1964.

5   The information on occupational stress contained in this chapter comes primarily from Selye, Hans, *The Stress of Life,* New York: McGraw-Hill Book Co., 1977. Particularly from the chapter entitled, "The Stressors of Daily Life," p. 369-395.

6   Rabkin and Struening, p. 1019.

7   Novak, Michael, "The Family Out of Favor." In Harper's Magazine, April, 1976, p. 38.

8   Rabkin and Struening, p. 1019.

9   See Ellerbroek, W.C., "Language, Thought, and Disease." In The Co-Evolution Quarterly, Spring 1978, p. 30-38.

10 *ibid,* p. 37.

11 Berger, Peter, *Invitation to Sociology: A Humanistic Perspective.* Garden City, New York: Doubleday and Company, Inc., 1963, p. 143.

12 *ibid*

13 Pelletier, Kenneth R., *Mind as Healer Mind as Slayer.* New York: Dell Publishing Co., 1977, p. 96.

14 *ibid*

15 Campbell, Joseph, *The Hero With a Thousand Faces.* New Jersey: Princeton University Press, 1973, p. 337.

CHAPTER V

1. This term is introduced by N. Author Coulter in his book, *Synergetics: An Adventure in Human Development.* Englewood Cliffs, New Jersey: Prentice-Hall, Inc., 1976, p. 82-83.

2. Alcoholic binges and excessive reading of escape literature are two pain drain examples offered by Coulter, p. 83.

3. Solomon, Richard L. and Corbit, John D., An Opponent-Process Theory of Motivation: I. Temporal Dynamics of Affect. Psychological Review, 81, 1974, p. 119-145.

4. *ibid,* p. 123.

5. *ibid,* p. 138.

6. The notion of "status addiction" is developed by Tibor Scitovsky in his book, *The Joyless Economy.* New York: Oxford University Press, 1976, p. 130-131.

7. *ibid,* p. 131.

8. The ideas developed in this paragraph come from Coulter, p. 32. He calls it the Analytical Principle of Synergetics. It reads: "…optimum development of the rational (analytic) mind of a human being will occur as a result of the rational application of knowledge about that mind to its own development."

9. Becker, Ernest, *Escape From Evil.* New York: The Free Press, 1975, p. 37.

10. Emerson, Ralph Waldo, *Heroism.* In Essays, Boston and New York: Houghton, Mifflin and Co., 1876, p. 245.

11. A brilliant analysis of scapegoating is offered by Becker, P. 109-114.

12. Vonnegut, Kurt, *Mother Night.* New York: Delacarte Press, 1966.

13. I owe this analysis to hours of discussion with Guy Cornwell, a highly decorated combat soldier from the Vietnam War.

14. Nock, Albert J., *Memoirs of a Superfluous Man.* New York: A.M.S. Press, 1943.

15. This exercise is drawn largely from the work of Jerome Lund, PhD. See *The Last Self-Help Book (Before Getting Results).* San Francisco: The Barclay Press, 1983.

16. This quote if form Ken Carey's book, *Starseed Transmission.*

APPENDIX A:

Answer Key for Progress Checks

CHAPTER I

1. absence of muscular tension, increased peripheral blood flow, quiet, non-active mind
2. anti-stress
3. cope
4. energy
5. disease
6. adaptation
7. more
8. adjust
9. two
10. weaknesses
11. weakest
12. stress
13. lifestyle
14. lifestyle
15. lower

CHAPTER II

1. once
2. tense-relax
3. sensations
4. 5, 0
5. relaxed
6. sensations
7. passive
8. detachment
9. least
10. comfortable
11. sitting, lying, reclining
12. eyes
13. habit
14. Evaluation
15. I
16. factors, issues

CHAPTER III

1. a quiet, non-active mind; scanning the body for signs of tension; deliberate

      living/ intentional doing
2. properly
3. deliberate or intentional
4. unintended
5. one
6. posture
7. mechanical
8. strain
9. organic
10. produced
11. deliberate
12. mini-challenges
13. normal or daily
14. "I could if I had to"
15. decided to
16. major

CHAPTER IV

1. anxiety or tension
2. stressful
3. strain
4. behaviors
5. situational
6. social
7. personal
8. curriculum or list
9. satisfied
12. love
13. love
14. stressful
15. Pleasing, Blaming, Computer, Irrelevant, Leveling
16. Leveling

CHAPTER V

1. mind
2. weakness/limitation
3. heroic
4. escape or avoid
5. addiction
6. add
7. ease
8. like
10. scapegoating
11. past
12. forgiveness
13. responsibility
14. conscious
15. one

APPENDIX B

The Relaxation Script

To create your own relaxation tape or CD, read the relaxation instructions with a deliberate and calm tone, pausing long enough with each set of instructions to allow 1) the muscles to be tensed, 2) the tension to be sensed and then released, and 3) the relaxation to be experienced. *(If you don't want to hear your own voice on the tape, ask someone who you think will do a good job, whose voice is soothing, for example.)*

When using the tape/CD, find a quiet, secluded place free of distractions. Assume a comfortable position, either lying on your back, sitting in a reclining chair, or sitting upright with your feet flat on the floor, your back straight. Remember to loosen your collar and belt, take off your glasses/remove your contacts, rest your hands comfortably in your lap or on the arms of the chair.

The task, once the tape begins, is to focus on the sensations coming from within your body. To facilitate this, begin with your eyes closed.

INSTRUCTIONS FOR RELAXATION TAPE (Read in a calm, deliberate manner):

What follows are a series of exercises sequenced so as to permit you to become profoundly relaxed. As you proceed, listen only to the instructions while attending carefully to the sensations coming from within your body. Remember that the next few minutes belong only to you. And remember also that you have chosen to relax, and to relax deeply.

Curl your toes as tightly as you can.
Notice the effect on your arches . . . your calves . . .
perhaps even your thighs.
Focus on the tension.
Hold it and when I say "Now," relax it.
Now.
And notice the difference.

Bend your toes back the other direction as far as you can,
and again, notice the effect on your arches . . . on the top of your feet . . .
and on your calves.
Hold it. Focus on it. *Now.* Relax it away.

Tighten your thighs. Make them as hard as you can.
Make them very hard and very tight.

Localize the tension. Make contact with the tension.
Hold it.
Now. Release it.

Tighten your hips. Make them as hard as you can.
Notice the discomfort.
Keep your legs relaxed if you can.
Localize the tension.
Hold it.
Now. Release it—relaxing you hips, thighs and feet.

Tighten your stomach as
if you were about to be hit in the stomach.
Make it very hard.
Notice the discomfort.
Legs relaxed.
Hold it.
Now.
And notice the difference.

Stick you stomach out as far as you can against your belt.
Make it as full as you can.
Stretch it.
Notice *that* discomfort.
Hold it. Focus on it.
Now, release it.

Tighten your fists, both of them as hard as you can.
Very tight. Notice how your fingers dig into the palms of your hands;
how the skin is stretched across your knuckles.
Notice the effect also on your forearms—perhaps even your upper arms.
Hold it. Very tight. Focus on it.
Stomach relaxed.
Now.
And notice the difference.

Bend your arms at your elbows and tighten your biceps.
Make them into knots. Hold the tension.
Stomach relaxed.
Very tight.
Focus on it. Hold it.
Now.
And notice the difference.
Allow your arms to relax all the way.

Raise your shoulders as high as you can, shrugging them.
Notice the tension in your upper back and in your neck.
Hold it.
Notice the discomfort.
Very tight.
Hands relaxed. Stomach relaxed.
Hold it,
Now.
Relax them all the way.

Turn your head all the way to the left,
tightening the muscles on one side of your neck while stretching
the muscles on the other side. All the way.
Feel it. *Stomach relaxed.* Hold it.
Now.

Turn your head the other direction,
stretching and tightening the opposite muscles.
Hold it. Focus on it.
Make mental contact with that tension.
And *Now*, release it.

Bring your chin to your chest,
Stretching the muscles in the back of your neck
and upper back.
Stretch them.
Hold it.
Focus on it.
Now.

Bite down—tighten your jaw—clenching your teeth.
Notice the effect on the muscles of your face.
Hold it. Feel it.
Very tight.
Now. Release it.

Push your tongue against the roof of your mouth.
Notice the effect on your tongue muscles.
Make your tongue very hard.
Hold it. Keep it there.
Stomach relaxed, hands relaxed.
Now . . . allowing your tongue to relax and widen.

Open your mouth as wide as you can—
stretching your cheeks.

Now stretch your lips even further by baring your teeth.
Very wide. Focus on the feeling.
Stomach and hands relaxed.
Hold it.
Now.
And notice the very big difference.

Bring your eyebrows together and frown, making as many
vertical wrinkles as you can on your forehead.
Notice *tha*t discomfort, that pain.
Hold it. Focus on it.
Now.
Release it, all the way.

Raise your eyebrows as high as you can, making as many
horizontal wrinkles as you can.
Eyebrows as high as you can. Hold it.
Notice the effect on your face.
Hold it. Very high.
Now.
Relax them,
smoothing out your forehead all the way.

With your eyes closed, move your eyeballs
all the way to the right.
Not so far that it hurts, but far enough to feel it.
Now.

And now your eyeballs to the left.
Now.

With your eyelids closed, raise your eyeballs as high as you can,
as though you were looking at something at the top of your forehead.
Inhale deeply and hold it. Hold it.
When I say "Now," let your eyes come to a comfortable position,
eyes closed, and exhale.
Now.

Take note of the various muscles of your body as I mention them,
making sure they are relaxed and that there is no tension.
First, your feet.
And now your calves.
Your thighs.
Hips.
Stomach.

Hands.
Arms.
Shoulders.
Neck.
And face.
No expression at all on your face.

And with each count allow yourself to become more deeply relaxed.
Moving from a *five* to a *four*.
And now, *three*.
Two.
Very deep, *one*.
Now all the way. . . *zero*.

Feeling very, very deeply relaxed but still alert and aware.

Enjoy this very deep level of relaxation for a while in silence.
(Pause for five to ten minutes.)

Is it possible for you to find zero, to come now to *zero*.
Allow this relaxed, calm feeling to stay
with you the rest of the day.
And come now, very gradually, from *zero* to *one*.
And now, *two*.
Three.
Feeling very relaxed, very calm, all the way to *four*.
Keep your eyes closed and come all the way back to *five*.

Feeling very good--
inhale deeply and hold it.
Hold it.
When I say "Now," exhale, open your eyes,
move your fingers and toes.
Now.

Sit quietly for a moment and take note of how you feel.

(Note: These instructions are a variation on the Progressive Relaxation
exercises developed by Edmund Jacobson.)

APPENDIX C

A Thirty-day Schedule —

Appendix C provides thirty days of relaxation schedules and evaluation forms. Schedule one relaxation session a day and as you complete each session, evaluate your experience.

If you miss a day here and there, that is understandable. Don't worry about it. But do get back on your schedule as soon as possible. The forms are provided to help you make a priority of daily practice.

As you proceed, attempt after a week or so to profoundly relax without the use of the tape/CD. Toward the end of the thirty days, when attempting to relax without the tape/CD, see if you can profoundly relax with fewer of the tense-relax exercises. The tape/CD will be there as you need it, but freeing you from your reliance on it is one of the goals of training.

RELAXATION SCHEDULE

Day: _____   Date: _____

	Time	Location	Position	Arrangements
8:00 – 8:30				
8:30 – 9:00				
9:00 – 9:30				
9:30 – 10:00				
10:00 – 10:30				
10:30 – 11:00				
11:00 – 11:30				
11:30 – 12:00				
12:00 – 12:30				
12:30 – 1:00				
1:00 – 1:30				
1:30 – 2:00				
2:00 – 2:30				
2:30 – 3:00				
3:00 – 3:30				
3:30 – 4:00				
4:00 – 4:30				
4:30 – 5:00				
5:00 – 5:30				
5:30 – 6:00				
6:00 – 6:30				
6:30 – 7:00				
7:00 – 7:30				
7:30 – 8:00				
8:00 – 8:30				
8:30 – 9:00				
9:00 – 9:30				
9:30 – 10:00				

RELAXATION SESSION EVALUATION FORM

During the relaxation session, I experienced the following:

Column I		Column II	
brief feelings of panic		restful alertness	
anxiety		saliva increase	
vulnerability		sudden muscle twitches	
frustration or irritability		heaviness in arms	
sadness or depression		heaviness in legs	
unpleasant thoughts		numbness in arms or legs	
feeling of being closed in		warmth in arms or legs	
desire to end session		warmth all over	
sexual worries		tingling sensations	
thoughts on commitments		heart pounding	
erratic breathing		awareness of breathing	
tearing from eyes		feelings of detachment	
tightness in throat or chest		physical relaxation	
cold hands		floating/drifting sensations	
tension in arms or legs		forgotten memories	
feeling of losing control		unusual images	
		fleeting images	
What in my life is responsible for the check marks in Column I?		vivid and static images	
		vivid and moving images	
		feelings of "letting go"	
		mental relaxation	
		pleasant feelings	
		calmness	
		joy or euphoria	

Using the scale below, I rate the depth of relaxation obtained during the relaxation session at the following level: _____

    5 – no more relaxed than when I started
    4 – more relaxed than when I started
    3 – relaxed
    2 – very relaxed
    1 – deeply relaxed
    0 – completely and thoroughly relaxed, calm and peaceful (profoundly relaxed)

RELAXATION SCHEDULE

Day: _____   Date: _____

	Time	Location	Position	Arrangements
8:00 – 8:30				
8:30 – 9:00				
9:00 – 9:30				
9:30 – 10:00				
10:00 – 10:30				
10:30 – 11:00				
11:00 – 11:30				
11:30 – 12:00				
12:00 – 12:30				
12:30 – 1:00				
1:00 – 1:30				
1:30 – 2:00				
2:00 – 2:30				
2:30 – 3:00				
3:00 – 3:30				
3:30 – 4:00				
4:00 – 4:30				
4:30 – 5:00				
5:00 – 5:30				
5:30 – 6:00				
6:00 – 6:30				
6:30 – 7:00				
7:00 – 7:30				
7:30 – 8:00				
8:00 – 8:30				
8:30 – 9:00				
9:00 – 9:30				
9:30 – 10:00				

RELAXATION SESSION EVALUATION FORM

During the relaxation session, I experienced the following:

Column I		Column II	
brief feelings of panic		restful alertness	
anxiety		saliva increase	
vulnerability		sudden muscle twitches	
frustration or irritability		heaviness in arms	
sadness or depression		heaviness in legs	
unpleasant thoughts		numbness in arms or legs	
feeling of being closed in		warmth in arms or legs	
desire to end session		warmth all over	
sexual worries		tingling sensations	
thoughts on commitments		heart pounding	
erratic breathing		awareness of breathing	
tearing from eyes		feelings of detachment	
tightness in throat or chest		physical relaxation	
cold hands		floating/drifting sensations	
tension in arms or legs		forgotten memories	
feeling of losing control		unusual images	
		fleeting images	
What in my life is responsible for the check marks in Column I?		vivid and static images	
		vivid and moving images	
		feelings of "letting go"	
		mental relaxation	
		pleasant feelings	
		calmness	
		joy or euphoria	

Using the scale below, I rate the depth of relaxation obtained during the relaxation session at the following level: _____

    5 – no more relaxed than when I started
    4 – more relaxed than when I started
    3 – relaxed
    2 – very relaxed
    1 – deeply relaxed
    0 – completely and thoroughly relaxed, calm and peaceful (profoundly relaxed)

RELAXATION SCHEDULE

Day: _____   Date: _____

	Time	Location	Position	Arrangements
8:00 – 8:30				
8:30 – 9:00				
9:00 – 9:30				
9:30 – 10:00				
10:00 – 10:30				
10:30 – 11:00				
11:00 – 11:30				
11:30 – 12:00				
12:00 – 12:30				
12:30 – 1:00				
1:00 – 1:30				
1:30 – 2:00				
2:00 – 2:30				
2:30 – 3:00				
3:00 – 3:30				
3:30 – 4:00				
4:00 – 4:30				
4:30 – 5:00				
5:00 – 5:30				
5:30 – 6:00				
6:00 – 6:30				
6:30 – 7:00				
7:00 – 7:30				
7:30 – 8:00				
8:00 – 8:30				
8:30 – 9:00				
9:00 – 9:30				
9:30 – 10:00				

RELAXATION SESSION EVALUATION FORM

During the relaxation session, I experienced the following:

Column I		Column II	
brief feelings of panic		restful alertness	
anxiety		saliva increase	
vulnerability		sudden muscle twitches	
frustration or irritability		heaviness in arms	
sadness or depression		heaviness in legs	
unpleasant thoughts		numbness in arms or legs	
feeling of being closed in		warmth in arms or legs	
desire to end session		warmth all over	
sexual worries		tingling sensations	
thoughts on commitments		heart pounding	
erratic breathing		awareness of breathing	
tearing from eyes		feelings of detachment	
tightness in throat or chest		physical relaxation	
cold hands		floating/drifting sensations	
tension in arms or legs		forgotten memories	
feeling of losing control		unusual images	
		fleeting images	
What in my life is responsible for the check marks in Column I?		vivid and static images	
		vivid and moving images	
		feelings of "letting go"	
		mental relaxation	
		pleasant feelings	
		calmness	
		joy or euphoria	

Using the scale below, I rate the depth of relaxation obtained during the relaxation session at the following level: _____

    5 – no more relaxed than when I started
    4 – more relaxed than when I started
    3 – relaxed
    2 – very relaxed
    1 – deeply relaxed
    0 – completely and thoroughly relaxed, calm and peaceful (profoundly relaxed)

RELAXATION SCHEDULE

Day: _____   Date: _____

	Time	Location	Position	Arrangements
8:00 – 8:30				
8:30 – 9:00				
9:00 – 9:30				
9:30 – 10:00				
10:00 – 10:30				
10:30 – 11:00				
11:00 – 11:30				
11:30 – 12:00				
12:00 – 12:30				
12:30 – 1:00				
1:00 – 1:30				
1:30 – 2:00				
2:00 – 2:30				
2:30 – 3:00				
3:00 – 3:30				
3:30 – 4:00				
4:00 – 4:30				
4:30 – 5:00				
5:00 – 5:30				
5:30 – 6:00				
6:00 – 6:30				
6:30 – 7:00				
7:00 – 7:30				
7:30 – 8:00				
8:00 – 8:30				
8:30 – 9:00				
9:00 – 9:30				
9:30 – 10:00				

RELAXATION SESSION EVALUATION FORM

During the relaxation session, I experienced the following:

Column I		Column II	
brief feelings of panic		restful alertness	
anxiety		saliva increase	
vulnerability		sudden muscle twitches	
frustration or irritability		heaviness in arms	
sadness or depression		heaviness in legs	
unpleasant thoughts		numbness in arms or legs	
feeling of being closed in		warmth in arms or legs	
desire to end session		warmth all over	
sexual worries		tingling sensations	
thoughts on commitments		heart pounding	
erratic breathing		awareness of breathing	
tearing from eyes		feelings of detachment	
tightness in throat or chest		physical relaxation	
cold hands		floating/drifting sensations	
tension in arms or legs		forgotten memories	
feeling of losing control		unusual images	
		fleeting images	
What in my life is responsible for the check marks in Column I?		vivid and static images	
		vivid and moving images	
		feelings of "letting go"	
		mental relaxation	
		pleasant feelings	
		calmness	
		joy or euphoria	

Using the scale below, I rate the depth of relaxation obtained during the relaxation session at the following level: _____

    5 – no more relaxed than when I started
    4 – more relaxed than when I started
    3 – relaxed
    2 – very relaxed
    1 – deeply relaxed
    0 – completely and thoroughly relaxed, calm and peaceful (profoundly relaxed)

RELAXATION SCHEDULE

Day: _____   Date: _____

	Time	Location	Position	Arrangements
8:00 – 8:30				
8:30 – 9:00				
9:00 – 9:30				
9:30 – 10:00				
10:00 – 10:30				
10:30 – 11:00				
11:00 – 11:30				
11:30 – 12:00				
12:00 – 12:30				
12:30 – 1:00				
1:00 – 1:30				
1:30 – 2:00				
2:00 – 2:30				
2:30 – 3:00				
3:00 – 3:30				
3:30 – 4:00				
4:00 – 4:30				
4:30 – 5:00				
5:00 – 5:30				
5:30 – 6:00				
6:00 – 6:30				
6:30 – 7:00				
7:00 – 7:30				
7:30 – 8:00				
8:00 – 8:30				
8:30 – 9:00				
9:00 – 9:30				
9:30 – 10:00				

RELAXATION SESSION EVALUATION FORM

During the relaxation session, I experienced the following:

Column I		Column II	
brief feelings of panic		restful alertness	
anxiety		saliva increase	
vulnerability		sudden muscle twitches	
frustration or irritability		heaviness in arms	
sadness or depression		heaviness in legs	
unpleasant thoughts		numbness in arms or legs	
feeling of being closed in		warmth in arms or legs	
desire to end session		warmth all over	
sexual worries		tingling sensations	
thoughts on commitments		heart pounding	
erratic breathing		awareness of breathing	
tearing from eyes		feelings of detachment	
tightness in throat or chest		physical relaxation	
cold hands		floating/drifting sensations	
tension in arms or legs		forgotten memories	
feeling of losing control		unusual images	
		fleeting images	
What in my life is responsible for the check marks in Column I?		vivid and static images	
		vivid and moving images	
		feelings of "letting go"	
		mental relaxation	
		pleasant feelings	
		calmness	
		joy or euphoria	

Using the scale below, I rate the depth of relaxation obtained during the relaxation session at the following level: _____

    5 – no more relaxed than when I started
    4 – more relaxed than when I started
    3 – relaxed
    2 – very relaxed
    1 – deeply relaxed
    0 – completely and thoroughly relaxed, calm and peaceful (profoundly relaxed)

RELAXATION SCHEDULE

Day: _____ Date: _____

Time	Location	Position	Arrangements
8:00 – 8:30			
8:30 – 9:00			
9:00 – 9:30			
9:30 – 10:00			
10:00 – 10:30			
10:30 – 11:00			
11:00 – 11:30			
11:30 – 12:00			
12:00 – 12:30			
12:30 – 1:00			
1:00 – 1:30			
1:30 – 2:00			
2:00 – 2:30			
2:30 – 3:00			
3:00 – 3:30			
3:30 – 4:00			
4:00 – 4:30			
4:30 – 5:00			
5:00 – 5:30			
5:30 – 6:00			
6:00 – 6:30			
6:30 – 7:00			
7:00 – 7:30			
7:30 – 8:00			
8:00 – 8:30			
8:30 – 9:00			
9:00 – 9:30			
9:30 – 10:00			

RELAXATION SESSION EVALUATION FORM

During the relaxation session, I experienced the following:

Column I		Column II	
brief feelings of panic		restful alertness	
anxiety		saliva increase	
vulnerability		sudden muscle twitches	
frustration or irritability		heaviness in arms	
sadness or depression		heaviness in legs	
unpleasant thoughts		numbness in arms or legs	
feeling of being closed in		warmth in arms or legs	
desire to end session		warmth all over	
sexual worries		tingling sensations	
thoughts on commitments		heart pounding	
erratic breathing		awareness of breathing	
tearing from eyes		feelings of detachment	
tightness in throat or chest		physical relaxation	
cold hands		floating/drifting sensations	
tension in arms or legs		forgotten memories	
feeling of losing control		unusual images	
		fleeting images	
What in my life is responsible for the check marks in Column I?		vivid and static images	
		vivid and moving images	
		feelings of "letting go"	
		mental relaxation	
		pleasant feelings	
		calmness	
		joy or euphoria	

Using the scale below, I rate the depth of relaxation obtained during the relaxation session at the following level: _____

    5 – no more relaxed than when I started
    4 – more relaxed than when I started
    3 – relaxed
    2 – very relaxed
    1 – deeply relaxed
    0 – completely and thoroughly relaxed, calm and peaceful (profoundly relaxed)

RELAXATION SCHEDULE

Day: _____   Date: _____

Time	Location	Position	Arrangements
8:00 – 8:30			
8:30 – 9:00			
9:00 – 9:30			
9:30 – 10:00			
10:00 – 10:30			
10:30 – 11:00			
11:00 – 11:30			
11:30 – 12:00			
12:00 – 12:30			
12:30 – 1:00			
1:00 – 1:30			
1:30 – 2:00			
2:00 – 2:30			
2:30 – 3:00			
3:00 – 3:30			
3:30 – 4:00			
4:00 – 4:30			
4:30 – 5:00			
5:00 – 5:30			
5:30 – 6:00			
6:00 – 6:30			
6:30 – 7:00			
7:00 – 7:30			
7:30 – 8:00			
8:00 – 8:30			
8:30 – 9:00			
9:00 – 9:30			
9:30 – 10:00			

RELAXATION SESSION EVALUATION FORM

During the relaxation session, I experienced the following:

Column I		Column II	
brief feelings of panic		restful alertness	
anxiety		saliva increase	
vulnerability		sudden muscle twitches	
frustration or irritability		heaviness in arms	
sadness or depression		heaviness in legs	
unpleasant thoughts		numbness in arms or legs	
feeling of being closed in		warmth in arms or legs	
desire to end session		warmth all over	
sexual worries		tingling sensations	
thoughts on commitments		heart pounding	
erratic breathing		awareness of breathing	
tearing from eyes		feelings of detachment	
tightness in throat or chest		physical relaxation	
cold hands		floating/drifting sensations	
tension in arms or legs		forgotten memories	
feeling of losing control		unusual images	
		fleeting images	
What in my life is responsible for the check marks in Column I?		vivid and static images	
		vivid and moving images	
		feelings of "letting go"	
		mental relaxation	
		pleasant feelings	
		calmness	
		joy or euphoria	

Using the scale below, I rate the depth of relaxation obtained during the relaxation session at the following level: _____

    5 – no more relaxed than when I started
    4 – more relaxed than when I started
    3 – relaxed
    2 – very relaxed
    1 – deeply relaxed
    0 – completely and thoroughly relaxed, calm and peaceful (profoundly relaxed)

RELAXATION SCHEDULE

Day: _____   Date: _____

	Time	Location	Position	Arrangements
8:00 – 8:30				
8:30 – 9:00				
9:00 – 9:30				
9:30 – 10:00				
10:00 – 10:30				
10:30 – 11:00				
11:00 – 11:30				
11:30 – 12:00				
12:00 – 12:30				
12:30 – 1:00				
1:00 – 1:30				
1:30 – 2:00				
2:00 – 2:30				
2:30 – 3:00				
3:00 – 3:30				
3:30 – 4:00				
4:00 – 4:30				
4:30 – 5:00				
5:00 – 5:30				
5:30 – 6:00				
6:00 – 6:30				
6:30 – 7:00				
7:00 – 7:30				
7:30 – 8:00				
8:00 – 8:30				
8:30 – 9:00				
9:00 – 9:30				
9:30 – 10:00				

RELAXATION SESSION EVALUATION FORM

During the relaxation session, I experienced the following:

Column I		Column II	
brief feelings of panic		restful alertness	
anxiety		saliva increase	
vulnerability		sudden muscle twitches	
frustration or irritability		heaviness in arms	
sadness or depression		heaviness in legs	
unpleasant thoughts		numbness in arms or legs	
feeling of being closed in		warmth in arms or legs	
desire to end session		warmth all over	
sexual worries		tingling sensations	
thoughts on commitments		heart pounding	
erratic breathing		awareness of breathing	
tearing from eyes		feelings of detachment	
tightness in throat or chest		physical relaxation	
cold hands		floating/drifting sensations	
tension in arms or legs		forgotten memories	
feeling of losing control		unusual images	
		fleeting images	
What in my life is responsible for the check marks in Column I?		vivid and static images	
		vivid and moving images	
		feelings of "letting go"	
		mental relaxation	
		pleasant feelings	
		calmness	
		joy or euphoria	

Using the scale below, I rate the depth of relaxation obtained during the relaxation session at the following level: _____

    5 – no more relaxed than when I started
    4 – more relaxed than when I started
    3 – relaxed
    2 – very relaxed
    1 – deeply relaxed
    0 – completely and thoroughly relaxed, calm and peaceful (profoundly relaxed)

RELAXATION SCHEDULE

Day: _____   Date: _____

	Time	Location	Position	Arrangements
8:00 – 8:30				
8:30 – 9:00				
9:00 – 9:30				
9:30 – 10:00				
10:00 – 10:30				
10:30 – 11:00				
11:00 – 11:30				
11:30 – 12:00				
12:00 – 12:30				
12:30 – 1:00				
1:00 – 1:30				
1:30 – 2:00				
2:00 – 2:30				
2:30 – 3:00				
3:00 – 3:30				
3:30 – 4:00				
4:00 – 4:30				
4:30 – 5:00				
5:00 – 5:30				
5:30 – 6:00				
6:00 – 6:30				
6:30 – 7:00				
7:00 – 7:30				
7:30 – 8:00				
8:00 – 8:30				
8:30 – 9:00				
9:00 – 9:30				
9:30 – 10:00				

RELAXATION SESSION EVALUATION FORM

During the relaxation session, I experienced the following:

Column I		Column II	
brief feelings of panic		restful alertness	
anxiety		saliva increase	
vulnerability		sudden muscle twitches	
frustration or irritability		heaviness in arms	
sadness or depression		heaviness in legs	
unpleasant thoughts		numbness in arms or legs	
feeling of being closed in		warmth in arms or legs	
desire to end session		warmth all over	
sexual worries		tingling sensations	
thoughts on commitments		heart pounding	
erratic breathing		awareness of breathing	
tearing from eyes		feelings of detachment	
tightness in throat or chest		physical relaxation	
cold hands		floating/drifting sensations	
tension in arms or legs		forgotten memories	
feeling of losing control		unusual images	
		fleeting images	
What in my life is responsible for the check marks in Column I?		vivid and static images	
		vivid and moving images	
		feelings of "letting go"	
		mental relaxation	
		pleasant feelings	
		calmness	
		joy or euphoria	

Using the scale below, I rate the depth of relaxation obtained during the relaxation session at the following level: _____

    5 – no more relaxed than when I started
    4 – more relaxed than when I started
    3 – relaxed
    2 – very relaxed
    1 – deeply relaxed
    0 – completely and thoroughly relaxed, calm and peaceful (profoundly relaxed)

RELAXATION SCHEDULE

Day: _____   Date: _____

	Time	Location	Position	Arrangements
8:00 – 8:30				
8:30 – 9:00				
9:00 – 9:30				
9:30 – 10:00				
10:00 – 10:30				
10:30 – 11:00				
11:00 – 11:30				
11:30 – 12:00				
12:00 – 12:30				
12:30 – 1:00				
1:00 – 1:30				
1:30 – 2:00				
2:00 – 2:30				
2:30 – 3:00				
3:00 – 3:30				
3:30 – 4:00				
4:00 – 4:30				
4:30 – 5:00				
5:00 – 5:30				
5:30 – 6:00				
6:00 – 6:30				
6:30 – 7:00				
7:00 – 7:30				
7:30 – 8:00				
8:00 – 8:30				
8:30 – 9:00				
9:00 – 9:30				
9:30 – 10:00				

RELAXATION SESSION EVALUATION FORM

During the relaxation session, I experienced the following:

Column I		Column II	
brief feelings of panic		restful alertness	
anxiety		saliva increase	
vulnerability		sudden muscle twitches	
frustration or irritability		heaviness in arms	
sadness or depression		heaviness in legs	
unpleasant thoughts		numbness in arms or legs	
feeling of being closed in		warmth in arms or legs	
desire to end session		warmth all over	
sexual worries		tingling sensations	
thoughts on commitments		heart pounding	
erratic breathing		awareness of breathing	
tearing from eyes		feelings of detachment	
tightness in throat or chest		physical relaxation	
cold hands		floating/drifting sensations	
tension in arms or legs		forgotten memories	
feeling of losing control		unusual images	
		fleeting images	
What in my life is responsible for the check marks in Column I?		vivid and static images	
		vivid and moving images	
		feelings of "letting go"	
		mental relaxation	
		pleasant feelings	
		calmness	
		joy or euphoria	

Using the scale below, I rate the depth of relaxation obtained during the relaxation session at the following level: _____

    5 – no more relaxed than when I started
    4 – more relaxed than when I started
    3 – relaxed
    2 – very relaxed
    1 – deeply relaxed
    0 – completely and thoroughly relaxed, calm and peaceful (profoundly relaxed)

RELAXATION SCHEDULE

Day: _____   Date: _____

	Time	Location	Position	Arrangements
8:00 – 8:30				
8:30 – 9:00				
9:00 – 9:30				
9:30 – 10:00				
10:00 – 10:30				
10:30 – 11:00				
11:00 – 11:30				
11:30 – 12:00				
12:00 – 12:30				
12:30 – 1:00				
1:00 – 1:30				
1:30 – 2:00				
2:00 – 2:30				
2:30 – 3:00				
3:00 – 3:30				
3:30 – 4:00				
4:00 – 4:30				
4:30 – 5:00				
5:00 – 5:30				
5:30 – 6:00				
6:00 – 6:30				
6:30 – 7:00				
7:00 – 7:30				
7:30 – 8:00				
8:00 – 8:30				
8:30 – 9:00				
9:00 – 9:30				
9:30 – 10:00				

RELAXATION SESSION EVALUATION FORM

During the relaxation session, I experienced the following:

Column I		Column II	
brief feelings of panic		restful alertness	
anxiety		saliva increase	
vulnerability		sudden muscle twitches	
frustration or irritability		heaviness in arms	
sadness or depression		heaviness in legs	
unpleasant thoughts		numbness in arms or legs	
feeling of being closed in		warmth in arms or legs	
desire to end session		warmth all over	
sexual worries		tingling sensations	
thoughts on commitments		heart pounding	
erratic breathing		awareness of breathing	
tearing from eyes		feelings of detachment	
tightness in throat or chest		physical relaxation	
cold hands		floating/drifting sensations	
tension in arms or legs		forgotten memories	
feeling of losing control		unusual images	
		fleeting images	
What in my life is responsible for the check marks in Column I?		vivid and static images	
		vivid and moving images	
		feelings of "letting go"	
		mental relaxation	
		pleasant feelings	
		calmness	
		joy or euphoria	

Using the scale below, I rate the depth of relaxation obtained during the relaxation session at the following level: _____

    5 – no more relaxed than when I started
    4 – more relaxed than when I started
    3 – relaxed
    2 – very relaxed
    1 – deeply relaxed
    0 – completely and thoroughly relaxed, calm and peaceful (profoundly relaxed)

RELAXATION SCHEDULE

Day: _____   Date: _____

	Time	Location	Position	Arrangements
8:00 – 8:30				
8:30 – 9:00				
9:00 – 9:30				
9:30 – 10:00				
10:00 – 10:30				
10:30 – 11:00				
11:00 – 11:30				
11:30 – 12:00				
12:00 – 12:30				
12:30 – 1:00				
1:00 – 1:30				
1:30 – 2:00				
2:00 – 2:30				
2:30 – 3:00				
3:00 – 3:30				
3:30 – 4:00				
4:00 – 4:30				
4:30 – 5:00				
5:00 – 5:30				
5:30 – 6:00				
6:00 – 6:30				
6:30 – 7:00				
7:00 – 7:30				
7:30 – 8:00				
8:00 – 8:30				
8:30 – 9:00				
9:00 – 9:30				
9:30 – 10:00				

RELAXATION SESSION EVALUATION FORM

During the relaxation session, I experienced the following:

Column I		Column II	
brief feelings of panic		restful alertness	
anxiety		saliva increase	
vulnerability		sudden muscle twitches	
frustration or irritability		heaviness in arms	
sadness or depression		heaviness in legs	
unpleasant thoughts		numbness in arms or legs	
feeling of being closed in		warmth in arms or legs	
desire to end session		warmth all over	
sexual worries		tingling sensations	
thoughts on commitments		heart pounding	
erratic breathing		awareness of breathing	
tearing from eyes		feelings of detachment	
tightness in throat or chest		physical relaxation	
cold hands		floating/drifting sensations	
tension in arms or legs		forgotten memories	
feeling of losing control		unusual images	
		fleeting images	
What in my life is responsible for the check marks in Column I?		vivid and static images	
		vivid and moving images	
		feelings of "letting go"	
		mental relaxation	
		pleasant feelings	
		calmness	
		joy or euphoria	

Using the scale below, I rate the depth of relaxation obtained during the relaxation session at the following level: _____

    5 – no more relaxed than when I started
    4 – more relaxed than when I started
    3 – relaxed
    2 – very relaxed
    1 – deeply relaxed
    0 – completely and thoroughly relaxed, calm and peaceful (profoundly relaxed)

RELAXATION SCHEDULE

Day: _____   Date: _____

Time	Location	Position	Arrangements
8:00 – 8:30			
8:30 – 9:00			
9:00 – 9:30			
9:30 – 10:00			
10:00 – 10:30			
10:30 – 11:00			
11:00 – 11:30			
11:30 – 12:00			
12:00 – 12:30			
12:30 – 1:00			
1:00 – 1:30			
1:30 – 2:00			
2:00 – 2:30			
2:30 – 3:00			
3:00 – 3:30			
3:30 – 4:00			
4:00 – 4:30			
4:30 – 5:00			
5:00 – 5:30			
5:30 – 6:00			
6:00 – 6:30			
6:30 – 7:00			
7:00 – 7:30			
7:30 – 8:00			
8:00 – 8:30			
8:30 – 9:00			
9:00 – 9:30			
9:30 – 10:00			

RELAXATION SESSION EVALUATION FORM

During the relaxation session, I experienced the following:

Column I		Column II	
brief feelings of panic		restful alertness	
anxiety		saliva increase	
vulnerability		sudden muscle twitches	
frustration or irritability		heaviness in arms	
sadness or depression		heaviness in legs	
unpleasant thoughts		numbness in arms or legs	
feeling of being closed in		warmth in arms or legs	
desire to end session		warmth all over	
sexual worries		tingling sensations	
thoughts on commitments		heart pounding	
erratic breathing		awareness of breathing	
tearing from eyes		feelings of detachment	
tightness in throat or chest		physical relaxation	
cold hands		floating/drifting sensations	
tension in arms or legs		forgotten memories	
feeling of losing control		unusual images	
		fleeting images	
What in my life is responsible for the check marks in Column I?		vivid and static images	
		vivid and moving images	
		feelings of "letting go"	
		mental relaxation	
		pleasant feelings	
		calmness	
		joy or euphoria	

Using the scale below, I rate the depth of relaxation obtained during the relaxation session at the following level: _____

5 – no more relaxed than when I started
4 – more relaxed than when I started
3 – relaxed
2 – very relaxed
1 – deeply relaxed
0 – completely and thoroughly relaxed, calm and peaceful (profoundly relaxed)

RELAXATION SCHEDULE

Day: _____   Date: _____

	Time	Location	Position	Arrangements
8:00 – 8:30				
8:30 – 9:00				
9:00 – 9:30				
9:30 – 10:00				
10:00 – 10:30				
10:30 – 11:00				
11:00 – 11:30				
11:30 – 12:00				
12:00 – 12:30				
12:30 – 1:00				
1:00 – 1:30				
1:30 – 2:00				
2:00 – 2:30				
2:30 – 3:00				
3:00 – 3:30				
3:30 – 4:00				
4:00 – 4:30				
4:30 – 5:00				
5:00 – 5:30				
5:30 – 6:00				
6:00 – 6:30				
6:30 – 7:00				
7:00 – 7:30				
7:30 – 8:00				
8:00 – 8:30				
8:30 – 9:00				
9:00 – 9:30				
9:30 – 10:00				

RELAXATION SESSION EVALUATION FORM

During the relaxation session, I experienced the following:

Column I		Column II	
brief feelings of panic		restful alertness	
anxiety		saliva increase	
vulnerability		sudden muscle twitches	
frustration or irritability		heaviness in arms	
sadness or depression		heaviness in legs	
unpleasant thoughts		numbness in arms or legs	
feeling of being closed in		warmth in arms or legs	
desire to end session		warmth all over	
sexual worries		tingling sensations	
thoughts on commitments		heart pounding	
erratic breathing		awareness of breathing	
tearing from eyes		feelings of detachment	
tightness in throat or chest		physical relaxation	
cold hands		floating/drifting sensations	
tension in arms or legs		forgotten memories	
feeling of losing control		unusual images	
		fleeting images	
What in my life is responsible for the check marks in Column I?		vivid and static images	
		vivid and moving images	
		feelings of "letting go"	
		mental relaxation	
		pleasant feelings	
		calmness	
		joy or euphoria	

Using the scale below, I rate the depth of relaxation obtained during the relaxation session at the following level: _____

        5 – no more relaxed than when I started
        4 – more relaxed than when I started
        3 – relaxed
        2 – very relaxed
        1 – deeply relaxed
        0 – completely and thoroughly relaxed, calm and peaceful (profoundly relaxed)

RELAXATION SCHEDULE

Day: _____   Date: _____

	Time	Location	Position	Arrangements
8:00 – 8:30				
8:30 – 9:00				
9:00 – 9:30				
9:30 – 10:00				
10:00 – 10:30				
10:30 – 11:00				
11:00 – 11:30				
11:30 – 12:00				
12:00 – 12:30				
12:30 – 1:00				
1:00 – 1:30				
1:30 – 2:00				
2:00 – 2:30				
2:30 – 3:00				
3:00 – 3:30				
3:30 – 4:00				
4:00 – 4:30				
4:30 – 5:00				
5:00 – 5:30				
5:30 – 6:00				
6:00 – 6:30				
6:30 – 7:00				
7:00 – 7:30				
7:30 – 8:00				
8:00 – 8:30				
8:30 – 9:00				
9:00 – 9:30				
9:30 – 10:00				

RELAXATION SESSION EVALUATION FORM

During the relaxation session, I experienced the following:

Column I		Column II	
brief feelings of panic		restful alertness	
anxiety		saliva increase	
vulnerability		sudden muscle twitches	
frustration or irritability		heaviness in arms	
sadness or depression		heaviness in legs	
unpleasant thoughts		numbness in arms or legs	
feeling of being closed in		warmth in arms or legs	
desire to end session		warmth all over	
sexual worries		tingling sensations	
thoughts on commitments		heart pounding	
erratic breathing		awareness of breathing	
tearing from eyes		feelings of detachment	
tightness in throat or chest		physical relaxation	
cold hands		floating/drifting sensations	
tension in arms or legs		forgotten memories	
feeling of losing control		unusual images	
		fleeting images	
What in my life is responsible for the check marks in Column I?		vivid and static images	
		vivid and moving images	
		feelings of "letting go"	
		mental relaxation	
		pleasant feelings	
		calmness	
		joy or euphoria	

Using the scale below, I rate the depth of relaxation obtained during the relaxation session at the following level: _____

    5 – no more relaxed than when I started
    4 – more relaxed than when I started
    3 – relaxed
    2 – very relaxed
    1 – deeply relaxed
    0 – completely and thoroughly relaxed, calm and peaceful (profoundly relaxed)

RELAXATION SCHEDULE

Day: _____   Date: _____

Time	Location	Position	Arrangements
8:00 – 8:30			
8:30 – 9:00			
9:00 – 9:30			
9:30 – 10:00			
10:00 – 10:30			
10:30 – 11:00			
11:00 – 11:30			
11:30 – 12:00			
12:00 – 12:30			
12:30 – 1:00			
1:00 – 1:30			
1:30 – 2:00			
2:00 – 2:30			
2:30 – 3:00			
3:00 – 3:30			
3:30 – 4:00			
4:00 – 4:30			
4:30 – 5:00			
5:00 – 5:30			
5:30 – 6:00			
6:00 – 6:30			
6:30 – 7:00			
7:00 – 7:30			
7:30 – 8:00			
8:00 – 8:30			
8:30 – 9:00			
9:00 – 9:30			
9:30 – 10:00			

RELAXATION SESSION EVALUATION FORM

During the relaxation session, I experienced the following:

Column I		Column II	
brief feelings of panic		restful alertness	
anxiety		saliva increase	
vulnerability		sudden muscle twitches	
frustration or irritability		heaviness in arms	
sadness or depression		heaviness in legs	
unpleasant thoughts		numbness in arms or legs	
feeling of being closed in		warmth in arms or legs	
desire to end session		warmth all over	
sexual worries		tingling sensations	
thoughts on commitments		heart pounding	
erratic breathing		awareness of breathing	
tearing from eyes		feelings of detachment	
tightness in throat or chest		physical relaxation	
cold hands		floating/drifting sensations	
tension in arms or legs		forgotten memories	
feeling of losing control		unusual images	
		fleeting images	
What in my life is responsible for the check marks in Column I?		vivid and static images	
		vivid and moving images	
		feelings of "letting go"	
		mental relaxation	
		pleasant feelings	
		calmness	
		joy or euphoria	

Using the scale below, I rate the depth of relaxation obtained during the relaxation session at the following level: _____

        5 – no more relaxed than when I started
        4 – more relaxed than when I started
        3 – relaxed
        2 – very relaxed
        1 – deeply relaxed
        0 – completely and thoroughly relaxed, calm and peaceful (profoundly relaxed)

RELAXATION SCHEDULE

Day: _____   Date: _____

	Time	Location	Position	Arrangements
8:00 – 8:30				
8:30 – 9:00				
9:00 – 9:30				
9:30 – 10:00				
10:00 – 10:30				
10:30 – 11:00				
11:00 – 11:30				
11:30 – 12:00				
12:00 – 12:30				
12:30 – 1:00				
1:00 – 1:30				
1:30 – 2:00				
2:00 – 2:30				
2:30 – 3:00				
3:00 – 3:30				
3:30 – 4:00				
4:00 – 4:30				
4:30 – 5:00				
5:00 – 5:30				
5:30 – 6:00				
6:00 – 6:30				
6:30 – 7:00				
7:00 – 7:30				
7:30 – 8:00				
8:00 – 8:30				
8:30 – 9:00				
9:00 – 9:30				
9:30 – 10:00				

RELAXATION SESSION EVALUATION FORM

During the relaxation session, I experienced the following:

Column I		Column II	
brief feelings of panic		restful alertness	
anxiety		saliva increase	
vulnerability		sudden muscle twitches	
frustration or irritability		heaviness in arms	
sadness or depression		heaviness in legs	
unpleasant thoughts		numbness in arms or legs	
feeling of being closed in		warmth in arms or legs	
desire to end session		warmth all over	
sexual worries		tingling sensations	
thoughts on commitments		heart pounding	
erratic breathing		awareness of breathing	
tearing from eyes		feelings of detachment	
tightness in throat or chest		physical relaxation	
cold hands		floating/drifting sensations	
tension in arms or legs		forgotten memories	
feeling of losing control		unusual images	
		fleeting images	
What in my life is responsible for the check marks in Column I?		vivid and static images	
		vivid and moving images	
		feelings of "letting go"	
		mental relaxation	
		pleasant feelings	
		calmness	
		joy or euphoria	

Using the scale below, I rate the depth of relaxation obtained during the relaxation session at the following level: _____

    5 – no more relaxed than when I started
    4 – more relaxed than when I started
    3 – relaxed
    2 – very relaxed
    1 – deeply relaxed
    0 – completely and thoroughly relaxed, calm and peaceful (profoundly relaxed)

RELAXATION SCHEDULE

Day: _____   Date: _____

Time	Time	Location	Position	Arrangements
8:00 – 8:30				
8:30 – 9:00				
9:00 – 9:30				
9:30 – 10:00				
10:00 – 10:30				
10:30 – 11:00				
11:00 – 11:30				
11:30 – 12:00				
12:00 – 12:30				
12:30 – 1:00				
1:00 – 1:30				
1:30 – 2:00				
2:00 – 2:30				
2:30 – 3:00				
3:00 – 3:30				
3:30 – 4:00				
4:00 – 4:30				
4:30 – 5:00				
5:00 – 5:30				
5:30 – 6:00				
6:00 – 6:30				
6:30 – 7:00				
7:00 – 7:30				
7:30 – 8:00				
8:00 – 8:30				
8:30 – 9:00				
9:00 – 9:30				
9:30 – 10:00				

RELAXATION SESSION EVALUATION FORM

During the relaxation session, I experienced the following:

Column I		Column II	
brief feelings of panic		restful alertness	
anxiety		saliva increase	
vulnerability		sudden muscle twitches	
frustration or irritability		heaviness in arms	
sadness or depression		heaviness in legs	
unpleasant thoughts		numbness in arms or legs	
feeling of being closed in		warmth in arms or legs	
desire to end session		warmth all over	
sexual worries		tingling sensations	
thoughts on commitments		heart pounding	
erratic breathing		awareness of breathing	
tearing from eyes		feelings of detachment	
tightness in throat or chest		physical relaxation	
cold hands		floating/drifting sensations	
tension in arms or legs		forgotten memories	
feeling of losing control		unusual images	
		fleeting images	
What in my life is responsible for the check marks in Column I?		vivid and static images	
		vivid and moving images	
		feelings of "letting go"	
		mental relaxation	
		pleasant feelings	
		calmness	
		joy or euphoria	

Using the scale below, I rate the depth of relaxation obtained during the relaxation session at the following level: _____

    5 – no more relaxed than when I started
    4 – more relaxed than when I started
    3 – relaxed
    2 – very relaxed
    1 – deeply relaxed
    0 – completely and thoroughly relaxed, calm and peaceful (profoundly relaxed)

RELAXATION SCHEDULE

Day: _____   Date: _____

Time	Location	Position	Arrangements
8:00 – 8:30			
8:30 – 9:00			
9:00 – 9:30			
9:30 – 10:00			
10:00 – 10:30			
10:30 – 11:00			
11:00 – 11:30			
11:30 – 12:00			
12:00 – 12:30			
12:30 – 1:00			
1:00 – 1:30			
1:30 – 2:00			
2:00 – 2:30			
2:30 – 3:00			
3:00 – 3:30			
3:30 – 4:00			
4:00 – 4:30			
4:30 – 5:00			
5:00 – 5:30			
5:30 – 6:00			
6:00 – 6:30			
6:30 – 7:00			
7:00 – 7:30			
7:30 – 8:00			
8:00 – 8:30			
8:30 – 9:00			
9:00 – 9:30			
9:30 – 10:00			

RELAXATION SESSION EVALUATION FORM

During the relaxation session, I experienced the following:

Column I		Column II	
brief feelings of panic		restful alertness	
anxiety		saliva increase	
vulnerability		sudden muscle twitches	
frustration or irritability		heaviness in arms	
sadness or depression		heaviness in legs	
unpleasant thoughts		numbness in arms or legs	
feeling of being closed in		warmth in arms or legs	
desire to end session		warmth all over	
sexual worries		tingling sensations	
thoughts on commitments		heart pounding	
erratic breathing		awareness of breathing	
tearing from eyes		feelings of detachment	
tightness in throat or chest		physical relaxation	
cold hands		floating/drifting sensations	
tension in arms or legs		forgotten memories	
feeling of losing control		unusual images	
		fleeting images	
What in my life is responsible for the check marks in Column I?		vivid and static images	
		vivid and moving images	
		feelings of "letting go"	
		mental relaxation	
		pleasant feelings	
		calmness	
		joy or euphoria	

Using the scale below, I rate the depth of relaxation obtained during the relaxation session at the following level: _____

  5 – no more relaxed than when I started
  4 – more relaxed than when I started
  3 – relaxed
  2 – very relaxed
  1 – deeply relaxed
  0 – completely and thoroughly relaxed, calm and peaceful (profoundly relaxed)

RELAXATION SCHEDULE

Day: _____   Date: _____

	Time	Location	Position	Arrangements
8:00 – 8:30				
8:30 – 9:00				
9:00 – 9:30				
9:30 – 10:00				
10:00 – 10:30				
10:30 – 11:00				
11:00 – 11:30				
11:30 – 12:00				
12:00 – 12:30				
12:30 – 1:00				
1:00 – 1:30				
1:30 – 2:00				
2:00 – 2:30				
2:30 – 3:00				
3:00 – 3:30				
3:30 – 4:00				
4:00 – 4:30				
4:30 – 5:00				
5:00 – 5:30				
5:30 – 6:00				
6:00 – 6:30				
6:30 – 7:00				
7:00 – 7:30				
7:30 – 8:00				
8:00 – 8:30				
8:30 – 9:00				
9:00 – 9:30				
9:30 – 10:00				

RELAXATION SESSION EVALUATION FORM

During the relaxation session, I experienced the following:

Column I		Column II	
brief feelings of panic		restful alertness	
anxiety		saliva increase	
vulnerability		sudden muscle twitches	
frustration or irritability		heaviness in arms	
sadness or depression		heaviness in legs	
unpleasant thoughts		numbness in arms or legs	
feeling of being closed in		warmth in arms or legs	
desire to end session		warmth all over	
sexual worries		tingling sensations	
thoughts on commitments		heart pounding	
erratic breathing		awareness of breathing	
tearing from eyes		feelings of detachment	
tightness in throat or chest		physical relaxation	
cold hands		floating/drifting sensations	
tension in arms or legs		forgotten memories	
feeling of losing control		unusual images	
		fleeting images	
What in my life is responsible for the check marks in Column I?		vivid and static images	
		vivid and moving images	
		feelings of "letting go"	
		mental relaxation	
		pleasant feelings	
		calmness	
		joy or euphoria	

Using the scale below, I rate the depth of relaxation obtained during the relaxation session at the following level: _____

    5 – no more relaxed than when I started
    4 – more relaxed than when I started
    3 – relaxed
    2 – very relaxed
    1 – deeply relaxed
    0 – completely and thoroughly relaxed, calm and peaceful (profoundly relaxed)

RELAXATION SCHEDULE

Day: _____   Date: _____

	Time	Location	Position	Arrangements
8:00 – 8:30				
8:30 – 9:00				
9:00 – 9:30				
9:30 – 10:00				
10:00 – 10:30				
10:30 – 11:00				
11:00 – 11:30				
11:30 – 12:00				
12:00 – 12:30				
12:30 – 1:00				
1:00 – 1:30				
1:30 – 2:00				
2:00 – 2:30				
2:30 – 3:00				
3:00 – 3:30				
3:30 – 4:00				
4:00 – 4:30				
4:30 – 5:00				
5:00 – 5:30				
5:30 – 6:00				
6:00 – 6:30				
6:30 – 7:00				
7:00 – 7:30				
7:30 – 8:00				
8:00 – 8:30				
8:30 – 9:00				
9:00 – 9:30				
9:30 – 10:00				

RELAXATION SESSION EVALUATION FORM

During the relaxation session, I experienced the following:

Column I		Column II	
brief feelings of panic		restful alertness	
anxiety		saliva increase	
vulnerability		sudden muscle twitches	
frustration or irritability		heaviness in arms	
sadness or depression		heaviness in legs	
unpleasant thoughts		numbness in arms or legs	
feeling of being closed in		warmth in arms or legs	
desire to end session		warmth all over	
sexual worries		tingling sensations	
thoughts on commitments		heart pounding	
erratic breathing		awareness of breathing	
tearing from eyes		feelings of detachment	
tightness in throat or chest		physical relaxation	
cold hands		floating/drifting sensations	
tension in arms or legs		forgotten memories	
feeling of losing control		unusual images	
		fleeting images	
What in my life is responsible for the check marks in Column I?		vivid and static images	
		vivid and moving images	
		feelings of "letting go"	
		mental relaxation	
		pleasant feelings	
		calmness	
		joy or euphoria	

Using the scale below, I rate the depth of relaxation obtained during the relaxation session at the following level: _____

    5 – no more relaxed than when I started
    4 – more relaxed than when I started
    3 – relaxed
    2 – very relaxed
    1 – deeply relaxed
    0 – completely and thoroughly relaxed, calm and peaceful (profoundly relaxed)

RELAXATION SCHEDULE

Day: _____   Date: _____

	Time	Location	Position	Arrangements
8:00 – 8:30				
8:30 – 9:00				
9:00 – 9:30				
9:30 – 10:00				
10:00 – 10:30				
10:30 – 11:00				
11:00 – 11:30				
11:30 – 12:00				
12:00 – 12:30				
12:30 – 1:00				
1:00 – 1:30				
1:30 – 2:00				
2:00 – 2:30				
2:30 – 3:00				
3:00 – 3:30				
3:30 – 4:00				
4:00 – 4:30				
4:30 – 5:00				
5:00 – 5:30				
5:30 – 6:00				
6:00 – 6:30				
6:30 – 7:00				
7:00 – 7:30				
7:30 – 8:00				
8:00 – 8:30				
8:30 – 9:00				
9:00 – 9:30				
9:30 – 10:00				

RELAXATION SESSION EVALUATION FORM

During the relaxation session, I experienced the following:

Column I		Column II	
brief feelings of panic		restful alertness	
anxiety		saliva increase	
vulnerability		sudden muscle twitches	
frustration or irritability		heaviness in arms	
sadness or depression		heaviness in legs	
unpleasant thoughts		numbness in arms or legs	
feeling of being closed in		warmth in arms or legs	
desire to end session		warmth all over	
sexual worries		tingling sensations	
thoughts on commitments		heart pounding	
erratic breathing		awareness of breathing	
tearing from eyes		feelings of detachment	
tightness in throat or chest		physical relaxation	
cold hands		floating/drifting sensations	
tension in arms or legs		forgotten memories	
feeling of losing control		unusual images	
		fleeting images	
What in my life is responsible for the check marks in Column I?		vivid and static images	
		vivid and moving images	
		feelings of "letting go"	
		mental relaxation	
		pleasant feelings	
		calmness	
		joy or euphoria	

Using the scale below, I rate the depth of relaxation obtained during the relaxation session at the following level: _____

    5 – no more relaxed than when I started
    4 – more relaxed than when I started
    3 – relaxed
    2 – very relaxed
    1 – deeply relaxed
    0 – completely and thoroughly relaxed, calm and peaceful (profoundly relaxed)

RELAXATION SCHEDULE

Day: _____   Date: _____

	Time	Location	Position	Arrangements
8:00 – 8:30				
8:30 – 9:00				
9:00 – 9:30				
9:30 – 10:00				
10:00 – 10:30				
10:30 – 11:00				
11:00 – 11:30				
11:30 – 12:00				
12:00 – 12:30				
12:30 – 1:00				
1:00 – 1:30				
1:30 – 2:00				
2:00 – 2:30				
2:30 – 3:00				
3:00 – 3:30				
3:30 – 4:00				
4:00 – 4:30				
4:30 – 5:00				
5:00 – 5:30				
5:30 – 6:00				
6:00 – 6:30				
6:30 – 7:00				
7:00 – 7:30				
7:30 – 8:00				
8:00 – 8:30				
8:30 – 9:00				
9:00 – 9:30				
9:30 – 10:00				

RELAXATION SESSION EVALUATION FORM

During the relaxation session, I experienced the following:

Column I		Column II	
brief feelings of panic		restful alertness	
anxiety		saliva increase	
vulnerability		sudden muscle twitches	
frustration or irritability		heaviness in arms	
sadness or depression		heaviness in legs	
unpleasant thoughts		numbness in arms or legs	
feeling of being closed in		warmth in arms or legs	
desire to end session		warmth all over	
sexual worries		tingling sensations	
thoughts on commitments		heart pounding	
erratic breathing		awareness of breathing	
tearing from eyes		feelings of detachment	
tightness in throat or chest		physical relaxation	
cold hands		floating/drifting sensations	
tension in arms or legs		forgotten memories	
feeling of losing control		unusual images	
		fleeting images	
What in my life is responsible for the check marks in Column I?		vivid and static images	
		vivid and moving images	
		feelings of "letting go"	
		mental relaxation	
		pleasant feelings	
		calmness	
		joy or euphoria	

Using the scale below, I rate the depth of relaxation obtained during the relaxation session at the following level: _____

    5 – no more relaxed than when I started
    4 – more relaxed than when I started
    3 – relaxed
    2 – very relaxed
    1 – deeply relaxed
    0 – completely and thoroughly relaxed, calm and peaceful (profoundly relaxed)

RELAXATION SCHEDULE

Day: _____   Date: _____

Time	Location	Position	Arrangements
8:00 – 8:30			
8:30 – 9:00			
9:00 – 9:30			
9:30 – 10:00			
10:00 – 10:30			
10:30 – 11:00			
11:00 – 11:30			
11:30 – 12:00			
12:00 – 12:30			
12:30 – 1:00			
1:00 – 1:30			
1:30 – 2:00			
2:00 – 2:30			
2:30 – 3:00			
3:00 – 3:30			
3:30 – 4:00			
4:00 – 4:30			
4:30 – 5:00			
5:00 – 5:30			
5:30 – 6:00			
6:00 – 6:30			
6:30 – 7:00			
7:00 – 7:30			
7:30 – 8:00			
8:00 – 8:30			
8:30 – 9:00			
9:00 – 9:30			
9:30 – 10:00			

RELAXATION SESSION EVALUATION FORM

During the relaxation session, I experienced the following:

Column I		Column II	
brief feelings of panic		restful alertness	
anxiety		saliva increase	
vulnerability		sudden muscle twitches	
frustration or irritability		heaviness in arms	
sadness or depression		heaviness in legs	
unpleasant thoughts		numbness in arms or legs	
feeling of being closed in		warmth in arms or legs	
desire to end session		warmth all over	
sexual worries		tingling sensations	
thoughts on commitments		heart pounding	
erratic breathing		awareness of breathing	
tearing from eyes		feelings of detachment	
tightness in throat or chest		physical relaxation	
cold hands		floating/drifting sensations	
tension in arms or legs		forgotten memories	
feeling of losing control		unusual images	
		fleeting images	
What in my life is responsible for the check marks in Column I?		vivid and static images	
		vivid and moving images	
		feelings of "letting go"	
		mental relaxation	
		pleasant feelings	
		calmness	
		joy or euphoria	

Using the scale below, I rate the depth of relaxation obtained during the relaxation session at the following level: _____

    5 – no more relaxed than when I started
    4 – more relaxed than when I started
    3 – relaxed
    2 – very relaxed
    1 – deeply relaxed
    0 – completely and thoroughly relaxed, calm and peaceful (profoundly relaxed)

RELAXATION SCHEDULE

Day: _____   Date: _____

	Time	Location	Position	Arrangements
8:00 – 8:30				
8:30 – 9:00				
9:00 – 9:30				
9:30 – 10:00				
10:00 – 10:30				
10:30 – 11:00				
11:00 – 11:30				
11:30 – 12:00				
12:00 – 12:30				
12:30 – 1:00				
1:00 – 1:30				
1:30 – 2:00				
2:00 – 2:30				
2:30 – 3:00				
3:00 – 3:30				
3:30 – 4:00				
4:00 – 4:30				
4:30 – 5:00				
5:00 – 5:30				
5:30 – 6:00				
6:00 – 6:30				
6:30 – 7:00				
7:00 – 7:30				
7:30 – 8:00				
8:00 – 8:30				
8:30 – 9:00				
9:00 – 9:30				
9:30 – 10:00				

RELAXATION SESSION EVALUATION FORM

During the relaxation session, I experienced the following:

Column I		Column II	
brief feelings of panic		restful alertness	
anxiety		saliva increase	
vulnerability		sudden muscle twitches	
frustration or irritability		heaviness in arms	
sadness or depression		heaviness in legs	
unpleasant thoughts		numbness in arms or legs	
feeling of being closed in		warmth in arms or legs	
desire to end session		warmth all over	
sexual worries		tingling sensations	
thoughts on commitments		heart pounding	
erratic breathing		awareness of breathing	
tearing from eyes		feelings of detachment	
tightness in throat or chest		physical relaxation	
cold hands		floating/drifting sensations	
tension in arms or legs		forgotten memories	
feeling of losing control		unusual images	
		fleeting images	
What in my life is responsible for the check marks in Column I?		vivid and static images	
		vivid and moving images	
		feelings of "letting go"	
		mental relaxation	
		pleasant feelings	
		calmness	
		joy or euphoria	

Using the scale below, I rate the depth of relaxation obtained during the relaxation session at the following level: _____

5 – no more relaxed than when I started
4 – more relaxed than when I started
3 – relaxed
2 – very relaxed
1 – deeply relaxed
0 – completely and thoroughly relaxed, calm and peaceful (profoundly relaxed)

RELAXATION SCHEDULE

Day: _____   Date: _____

Time	Location	Position	Arrangements
8:00 – 8:30			
8:30 – 9:00			
9:00 – 9:30			
9:30 – 10:00			
10:00 – 10:30			
10:30 – 11:00			
11:00 – 11:30			
11:30 – 12:00			
12:00 – 12:30			
12:30 – 1:00			
1:00 – 1:30			
1:30 – 2:00			
2:00 – 2:30			
2:30 – 3:00			
3:00 – 3:30			
3:30 – 4:00			
4:00 – 4:30			
4:30 – 5:00			
5:00 – 5:30			
5:30 – 6:00			
6:00 – 6:30			
6:30 – 7:00			
7:00 – 7:30			
7:30 – 8:00			
8:00 – 8:30			
8:30 – 9:00			
9:00 – 9:30			
9:30 – 10:00			

RELAXATION SESSION EVALUATION FORM

During the relaxation session, I experienced the following:

Column I		Column II	
brief feelings of panic		restful alertness	
anxiety		saliva increase	
vulnerability		sudden muscle twitches	
frustration or irritability		heaviness in arms	
sadness or depression		heaviness in legs	
unpleasant thoughts		numbness in arms or legs	
feeling of being closed in		warmth in arms or legs	
desire to end session		warmth all over	
sexual worries		tingling sensations	
thoughts on commitments		heart pounding	
erratic breathing		awareness of breathing	
tearing from eyes		feelings of detachment	
tightness in throat or chest		physical relaxation	
cold hands		floating/drifting sensations	
tension in arms or legs		forgotten memories	
feeling of losing control		unusual images	
		fleeting images	
What in my life is responsible for the check marks in Column I?		vivid and static images	
		vivid and moving images	
		feelings of "letting go"	
		mental relaxation	
		pleasant feelings	
		calmness	
		joy or euphoria	

Using the scale below, I rate the depth of relaxation obtained during the relaxation session at the following level: _____

    5 – no more relaxed than when I started
    4 – more relaxed than when I started
    3 – relaxed
    2 – very relaxed
    1 – deeply relaxed
    0 – completely and thoroughly relaxed, calm and peaceful (profoundly relaxed)

RELAXATION SCHEDULE

Day: _____   Date: _____

	Time	Location	Position	Arrangements
8:00 – 8:30				
8:30 – 9:00				
9:00 – 9:30				
9:30 – 10:00				
10:00 – 10:30				
10:30 – 11:00				
11:00 – 11:30				
11:30 – 12:00				
12:00 – 12:30				
12:30 – 1:00				
1:00 – 1:30				
1:30 – 2:00				
2:00 – 2:30				
2:30 – 3:00				
3:00 – 3:30				
3:30 – 4:00				
4:00 – 4:30				
4:30 – 5:00				
5:00 – 5:30				
5:30 – 6:00				
6:00 – 6:30				
6:30 – 7:00				
7:00 – 7:30				
7:30 – 8:00				
8:00 – 8:30				
8:30 – 9:00				
9:00 – 9:30				
9:30 – 10:00				

RELAXATION SESSION EVALUATION FORM

During the relaxation session, I experienced the following:

Column I		Column II	
brief feelings of panic		restful alertness	
anxiety		saliva increase	
vulnerability		sudden muscle twitches	
frustration or irritability		heaviness in arms	
sadness or depression		heaviness in legs	
unpleasant thoughts		numbness in arms or legs	
feeling of being closed in		warmth in arms or legs	
desire to end session		warmth all over	
sexual worries		tingling sensations	
thoughts on commitments		heart pounding	
erratic breathing		awareness of breathing	
tearing from eyes		feelings of detachment	
tightness in throat or chest		physical relaxation	
cold hands		floating/drifting sensations	
tension in arms or legs		forgotten memories	
feeling of losing control		unusual images	
		fleeting images	
What in my life is responsible for the check marks in Column I?		vivid and static images	
		vivid and moving images	
		feelings of "letting go"	
		mental relaxation	
		pleasant feelings	
		calmness	
		joy or euphoria	

Using the scale below, I rate the depth of relaxation obtained during the relaxation session at the following level: _____

    5 – no more relaxed than when I started
    4 – more relaxed than when I started
    3 – relaxed
    2 – very relaxed
    1 – deeply relaxed
    0 – completely and thoroughly relaxed, calm and peaceful (profoundly relaxed)

RELAXATION SCHEDULE

Day: _____   Date: _____

	Time	Location	Position	Arrangements
8:00 – 8:30				
8:30 – 9:00				
9:00 – 9:30				
9:30 – 10:00				
10:00 – 10:30				
10:30 – 11:00				
11:00 – 11:30				
11:30 – 12:00				
12:00 – 12:30				
12:30 – 1:00				
1:00 – 1:30				
1:30 – 2:00				
2:00 – 2:30				
2:30 – 3:00				
3:00 – 3:30				
3:30 – 4:00				
4:00 – 4:30				
4:30 – 5:00				
5:00 – 5:30				
5:30 – 6:00				
6:00 – 6:30				
6:30 – 7:00				
7:00 – 7:30				
7:30 – 8:00				
8:00 – 8:30				
8:30 – 9:00				
9:00 – 9:30				
9:30 – 10:00				

RELAXATION SESSION EVALUATION FORM

During the relaxation session, I experienced the following:

Column I		Column II	
brief feelings of panic		restful alertness	
anxiety		saliva increase	
vulnerability		sudden muscle twitches	
frustration or irritability		heaviness in arms	
sadness or depression		heaviness in legs	
unpleasant thoughts		numbness in arms or legs	
feeling of being closed in		warmth in arms or legs	
desire to end session		warmth all over	
sexual worries		tingling sensations	
thoughts on commitments		heart pounding	
erratic breathing		awareness of breathing	
tearing from eyes		feelings of detachment	
tightness in throat or chest		physical relaxation	
cold hands		floating/drifting sensations	
tension in arms or legs		forgotten memories	
feeling of losing control		unusual images	
		fleeting images	
What in my life is responsible for the check marks in Column I?		vivid and static images	
		vivid and moving images	
		feelings of "letting go"	
		mental relaxation	
		pleasant feelings	
		calmness	
		joy or euphoria	

Using the scale below, I rate the depth of relaxation obtained during the relaxation session at the following level: _____

    5 – no more relaxed than when I started
    4 – more relaxed than when I started
    3 – relaxed
    2 – very relaxed
    1 – deeply relaxed
    0 – completely and thoroughly relaxed, calm and peaceful (profoundly relaxed)

RELAXATION SCHEDULE

Day: _____   Date: _____

	Time	Location	Position	Arrangements
8:00 – 8:30				
8:30 – 9:00				
9:00 – 9:30				
9:30 – 10:00				
10:00 – 10:30				
10:30 – 11:00				
11:00 – 11:30				
11:30 – 12:00				
12:00 – 12:30				
12:30 – 1:00				
1:00 – 1:30				
1:30 – 2:00				
2:00 – 2:30				
2:30 – 3:00				
3:00 – 3:30				
3:30 – 4:00				
4:00 – 4:30				
4:30 – 5:00				
5:00 – 5:30				
5:30 – 6:00				
6:00 – 6:30				
6:30 – 7:00				
7:00 – 7:30				
7:30 – 8:00				
8:00 – 8:30				
8:30 – 9:00				
9:00 – 9:30				
9:30 – 10:00				

RELAXATION SESSION EVALUATION FORM

During the relaxation session, I experienced the following:

Column I		Column II	
brief feelings of panic		restful alertness	
anxiety		saliva increase	
vulnerability		sudden muscle twitches	
frustration or irritability		heaviness in arms	
sadness or depression		heaviness in legs	
unpleasant thoughts		numbness in arms or legs	
feeling of being closed in		warmth in arms or legs	
desire to end session		warmth all over	
sexual worries		tingling sensations	
thoughts on commitments		heart pounding	
erratic breathing		awareness of breathing	
tearing from eyes		feelings of detachment	
tightness in throat or chest		physical relaxation	
cold hands		floating/drifting sensations	
tension in arms or legs		forgotten memories	
feeling of losing control		unusual images	
		fleeting images	
What in my life is responsible for the check marks in Column I?		vivid and static images	
		vivid and moving images	
		feelings of "letting go"	
		mental relaxation	
		pleasant feelings	
		calmness	
		joy or euphoria	

Using the scale below, I rate the depth of relaxation obtained during the relaxation session at the following level: _____

5 – no more relaxed than when I started
4 – more relaxed than when I started
3 – relaxed
2 – very relaxed
1 – deeply relaxed
0 – completely and thoroughly relaxed, calm and peaceful (profoundly relaxed)

RELAXATION SCHEDULE

Day: _____   Date: _____

	Time	Location	Position	Arrangements
8:00 – 8:30				
8:30 – 9:00				
9:00 – 9:30				
9:30 – 10:00				
10:00 – 10:30				
10:30 – 11:00				
11:00 – 11:30				
11:30 – 12:00				
12:00 – 12:30				
12:30 – 1:00				
1:00 – 1:30				
1:30 – 2:00				
2:00 – 2:30				
2:30 – 3:00				
3:00 – 3:30				
3:30 – 4:00				
4:00 – 4:30				
4:30 – 5:00				
5:00 – 5:30				
5:30 – 6:00				
6:00 – 6:30				
6:30 – 7:00				
7:00 – 7:30				
7:30 – 8:00				
8:00 – 8:30				
8:30 – 9:00				
9:00 – 9:30				
9:30 – 10:00				

RELAXATION SESSION EVALUATION FORM

During the relaxation session, I experienced the following:

Column I		Column II	
brief feelings of panic		restful alertness	
anxiety		saliva increase	
vulnerability		sudden muscle twitches	
frustration or irritability		heaviness in arms	
sadness or depression		heaviness in legs	
unpleasant thoughts		numbness in arms or legs	
feeling of being closed in		warmth in arms or legs	
desire to end session		warmth all over	
sexual worries		tingling sensations	
thoughts on commitments		heart pounding	
erratic breathing		awareness of breathing	
tearing from eyes		feelings of detachment	
tightness in throat or chest		physical relaxation	
cold hands		floating/drifting sensations	
tension in arms or legs		forgotten memories	
feeling of losing control		unusual images	
		fleeting images	
What in my life is responsible for the check marks in Column I?		vivid and static images	
		vivid and moving images	
		feelings of "letting go"	
		mental relaxation	
		pleasant feelings	
		calmness	
		joy or euphoria	

Using the scale below, I rate the depth of relaxation obtained during the relaxation session at the following level: _____

    5 – no more relaxed than when I started
    4 – more relaxed than when I started
    3 – relaxed
    2 – very relaxed
    1 – deeply relaxed
    0 – completely and thoroughly relaxed, calm and peaceful (profoundly relaxed)

www.ingramcontent.com/pod-product-compliance
Lightning Source LLC
Chambersburg PA
CBHW081154290426
44108CB00018B/2550